The Freedom Frequency

—Raise Your Vibration & Live Above the Line

Karen Klassen

The Freedom Frequency—Raise Your Vibration & Live
Above the Line

Editing by Tyler Tichelaar
Formatting by Larry Alexander
Cover Design by C Horton

For inquiries, please contact: Karen Klassen

www.womenembracingbrilliance.com

www.thefreedomfrequency.com

ISBN: 978-0-9918890-0-6

First Edition

To all the earth angels who are here to

co-create heaven on earth.

Acknowledgments

I am grateful to so many people who have been there through my most challenging times and who have supported me on my journey of awakening to my soul's purpose and passion.

Thank you to:

My dad for your unwavering belief, love, words of wisdom and for walking the spiritual path beside me.

My mom for being one of my greatest teachers on my path to unconditional love, and for always being there no matter how many times I fell down.

To my remarkable brother Dwayne for having the courage to stand beside me in the many storms of life, and to persevere continually with dedication and soul-driven purpose.

To Katharina for showing me the path of the feminine, for being a shining example of enlightened love, and for always being there no matter what.

To Laura for showing me what it means to have an unshakable determination, to live with purpose and passion and what it truly means to embrace the health vibration.

To Janice for being a living example of what it means to live in truth and for reminding me of my own brilliance in the moments I forgot.

To Krista for reflecting and expressing beauty, grace, and elegance in my life and showing me what is truly possible.

To Carol for generously sharing your knowledge, creativity and believing in my journey beyond the familiar.

And to my beloved Alan for his brave heart in saying yes to diving deep into his darkness and mirroring the forgotten parts of myself so I could fully embrace my divine feminine power.

Table of Contents

Introduction

I deeply love and appreciate my parents and I am grateful to my soul for saying "yes" to being birthed in such an environment so I could learn powerful life lessons.

To begin, I grew up in an authoritarian household governed by, "Do what I say; not what I do." As young as I was, I was frustrated with how my parents communicated by constantly yelling, pointing fingers, arguing about everything, and then avoiding each other for days. I desperately craved attention. I wanted to be heard and especially understood. I was called a crybaby every time I showed tears. I had no idea how to handle the conflicting energies between my parents and no matter what I said, I felt small and insecure.

I was a good kid which meant keeping my room clean, never talking back, doing what was asked of me, doing well in school, and never getting into trouble. My escape was spending all of my spare time riding my horse.

Everything of course began to change as I grew into a young rebellious teenager. My parents, especially my mother, began to transfer their unhappiness onto me. Having one parent yelling at me was challenging enough, but to have both parents joining forces in a barrage of cruel words was more than my young soul could bear. At the time, I did not have the understanding that my parents were using me as a scapegoat to transfer all the emotional pain alive inside of them.

I believe there is a defining moment where the ego veils the light of the soul. I remember the moment vividly. I was sitting on the floor while both my parents stood over me yelling and blaming me for their unhappiness. Up until that moment I had been a well-behaved kid but now everything would change.

In the midst of my deep sadness and tears I heard a voice, a voice that did not belong to my mom or dad. I listened again. To my surprise, it was coming from inside my head. The voice repeated so clearly there was no way I could misinterpret its message. The voice said, "Do you want me to take care of you?"

My parents continued to yell at me from above and now threatened to send me to a psychiatric hospital. Seriously, they wanted to send me away because I cried too much? The fear of being sent away, leaving the only family I knew, paralyzed my mind and my body. I had no idea how to cope with the situation. Was I crazy? Did crying make me a crazy person? The voice within spoke again, "Let me take care of you. I will make you strong."

I could not stop crying, and in the midst of the hurt and a longing to feel loved and accepted, I answered the voice with a "Yes." With permission granted, I instantly felt a rush of energy move through my body. I could not believe the power I was feeling. My tears instantly dried up. I felt different as if something had just taken over my body. I felt strong. This inner strength was incredible. I felt all fear vanish. I looked up at my parents and I was no longer afraid of them. They now just looked like two puppets on strings. I could see their mouths moving, but I could not hear their words. I slid my back up the wall. Now standing, I felt powerful. Invincible! A smile came over my face. I no longer cared what my parents thought or said to me as my love for them vanished into thin air. I no longer cared about anything. I felt so good. I felt free. I just looked at them both, smiled, and walked to my room. I grabbed my ghetto blaster, put in an ACDC cassette, and turned up the volume. Then I walked down the stairs, fingered them both, told them I hated them and was not coming back, and walked out.

I did come back physically, but they would never see that innocent little girl ever again. I enjoyed my newfound power for many years, as my Dark self possessed my life. It showed me the path of drugs, alcohol, and sex that would feed my inner demons. I was shown the power to manipulate, to hate, to resent, and to deceive. I discovered the power in pretending I was someone else. I could become the shy girl, an innocent girl, the bitch, or the slut. I was like a chameleon and I knew how to get my way. My light, my soul would be buried for many years as the destructive force within would create many walls around my heart, concealing the truth of who I am.

My inner demons (what I now refer to as my inner *Fallen Angels*) began to grow in strength and would create havoc in my life. I was kind to people only because I knew they had something I wanted. All I wanted to do was get high.

When I was nineteen, I was on welfare. I hated life. I know hate is a strong word but that was my state of mind at the time. I blamed everyone for my loneliness, for my suffering, and for the dull and mundane life I was living. I had already been raped twice and because I was so unconscious, I did not even see it as rape until much later in life. I hated my body. I was addicted to drugs and alcohol and I only associated with people who were as lost and alone as I was. In my twenties, I married an abusive drug dealer and was in a job that was unfulfilling. I suffered from chronic back pain, scoliosis, Irritable Bowel Syndrome, allergies, fatigue, depression, and continuous suicidal thoughts. Doctors told me that if I didn't change my life, I would be dead by the time I was thirty.

Thankfully, I had a spiritual awakening in 1993 or what I feel was a direct experience of Source. I was home sick and feeling sorry for myself. I had just watched Shirley MacLaine's movie, *Out on a Limb,* and was now contemplating my life. Questions I had never asked myself before began to surface such as, "Who Am I?" and "Why Am I Here?" Within moments, I felt the energy in my living room change. I felt a wave of energy wash over my body, intensifying with every second as if a lightning bolt were surging through every cell. I felt fear rise up briefly only to be replaced with a blanket of the most beautiful love; a love beyond anything I had ever known. I became aware of the part of me that was whole and had never experienced pain, harm, or suffering. I felt connected to all of life and knew my soul came to this beautiful planet for a higher purpose. Then, as fast as this defining moment emerged, it left leaving me dazed, confused, and wondering what had just happened?

As I looked around my living room, I could still feel the highly charged energy on my skin as every hair on my arms stood straight up. I felt different. I could see energy particles of light dancing in my living room.

I wanted to feel this profound love again. Then I heard a voice. Yes, another voice in my head, like a thought with the volume turned up. This voice felt different. With full clarity it said, "If you want to feel this love again, relinquish all fear that limits you."

Since that moment, my life immediately changed direction. Where once I could only see darkness, suffering, loss, and despair, I now saw the truth, the truth that all human beings have been given the divine power to create heaven on earth for themselves. If I were to experience heaven on earth for myself, I was to create heaven in my mind first.

I had a thirst, a hunger to know more. I began a journey beyond the familiar. I was on a quest of self-discovery as I had this persistent desire to feel and connect with this higher love again, a love I now call *Enlightened Love*. I knew this higher love would set me free of all the mental, emotional, and physical pain I was experiencing.

My purpose in writing this book is to share with you the journey I took in transforming my life from emotional, mental, and physical pain that nearly destroyed me, to living in the higher worlds of love and freedom. I will show you that by making small shifts in how you view yourself and the world around you, you can impact your life in profound ways. I will show you all the possibilities available and all you are asked to do is apply and integrate these higher ideas I offer.

I am not a doctor, a psychiatrist, or psychologist. I can only share my experiences with you and what has empowered me in becoming the woman I am today. Through many years of self-discipline and devotion to my spiritual calling, I was able to transform my once dis-eased body into a healthy body free from pain and drugs. I now live a life free of the many negative emotions and dark voices that once consumed me. I have attracted my beloved, a man who is not afraid of my feminine power, who is centered in his heart and lovingly supports everything I do. I have transformed my relationships with my parents and brother, and I now attract people in my life who vibrate in a higher frequency of love, collaboration, and respect.

I will introduce you to a whole new way of seeing your emotions. I will also show you how you can free yourself from perceived negative emotions and qualities that may be sabotaging your relationships or holding you back from experiencing the love and joy that is rightfully yours. In this book, I offer 80 Higher Ideas. Each one is to be used as a life guide or reference tool to empower you in your relationships and every area of your life. You are here to live above the line and connect to a higher intelligence that holds the blueprint to living in the Freedom Frequency of life.

As you read through, I will refer to *Selves* (upper case) as aspect of you that resonate above the line, in the Frequency of Freedom and *selves* (lower case) as aspects of you that resonate below the line, in the Frequency of Fear.

For each *Higher Idea*, I suggest you contemplate the words expressed and think of them as inspired action steps you can take right now. You can work through the *Higher Ideas* in order, or you can just open up this book any day of the week, and whatever page you open, you will find your own personal *Higher Idea* for that day.

If you commit to bringing each of these 80 Higher Ideas into your life, you will notice an incredible transformation as you spiral up and live above the line in the Freedom Frequency of life.

In the Spirit of Oneness,

Karen Klassen

Chapter One

Journey Beyond the Familiar

Are you ready to remember the truth of who you are? Are you ready to experience more fulfilling relationships where you are accepted for who you are? Are you ready to reclaim your power and stand for what you believe in? If you said, "Yes" to any of the above questions, then congratulations! You are ready to dive deep into the most fascinating journey you will ever take, *a journey beyond the familiar.*

We are in the midst of a planetary awakening where we are shifting from a fear-based world of stress, uncertainty, and anger to living above the line in the frequency of freedom of love, peace of mind, and abundance for all.

We all experience loss, pain, and suffering at some point in our lives. If we are open to learning our life lessons, we see that all experience is an opportunity for us to open our hearts to love, acceptance, and embrace a deeper truth. This book is for those who are ready to spiral up into living a heart-centered life.

I believe you are not flawed, you do not have faults, and you are not "just a human being." You are Divinely perfect just as you are. I believe we are all Divinely perfect. Perfection from an ego perspective is when we pretend we are happy and we do not tell the truth about how we feel or the problems we are facing. This is the opposite of Divine perfection.

1

Divine perfection is letting go of judgments about yourself. It means being truthful with yourself right here, right now in the moment and seeing that the YOU that is here, whether you are sad, afraid, happy, unfulfilled, laughing, angry or content *is* Divinely perfect. It is about being authentic and telling people what is going on truthfully. Only then can you spiral up to higher levels of consciousness.

I don't believe God made any mistakes and if you are created in the image of the Creator then you would be Divinely perfect. Every thought, word or experience you have had or are having, *is* in divine order for the awakening and evolution of your soul and all humanity.

You may have been taught to see yourself as small, imperfect and weak because you may not have your life all together. Who does? What if you stopped striving for perfection and instead could see that your soul is already Divinely perfect and that you are loved by the Universe no matter what. You are a gift to the world. You are *living art*. Everything is divinely orchestrated for you to wake up to the essence of who you really are – *a divine human being*.

The reason why there is so much misery, struggle, and tragedy in our lives is because we have forgotten this truth. We have separated ourselves from our own Divine natures. We fear the unknown because we don't know what it looks like, or we think we may not be loved and appreciated for who we will become. Why have we made our own happiness, freedom, and our *BIGNESS* something to be so afraid of? Another reason we hold ourselves back is the belief that if we choose *growth* and *spiritual fulfillment,* we will leave our loved ones behind. How about a higher idea that no one is ever left behind? Every soul is travelling on a unique journey beyond the familiar and will evolve at their own pace.

Every human being is on his or her spiritual path whether consciously aware of it or not. We are all moving through a spiritual metamorphosis, from living a fear-based life of anger, separation, and greed to a love-centered life of purpose, oneness, and abundance. This way of life is possible for all, and many people around the globe are already experiencing a heart-centered life.

The analogy of the caterpillar becoming a butterfly is often used to help us understand our own process of the life transformations we experience. In order to complete their metamorphoses into butterflies, caterpillars create a chrysalis where their cells begin to resonate at a higher frequency. Their current form breaks down as these new cells begin to resonate together into a genetic goop, leaving them extremely vulnerable. This vulnerability phase creates the space for something new to be birthed, the emergence of a butterfly. Just as the seed and evolutionary blueprint to transform exists within the caterpillar, the seed and evolutionary blueprint to transform from one identity to another exists within YOU.

You may be going through your own metamorphosis now, and it may feel like hell as you move through your own "goop of vulnerability." Remember, the caterpillar does not make itself into a butterfly. It seeks the butterfly within. When you seek your own Brilliant Self, your new cells begin to dissolve the "current you" automatically, without effort, only to reveal your wings of freedom.

Moving from where you are (your current reality) to where you want to be (preferred reality) involves a desire for personal and spiritual growth and a willingness to dive in and remember who you are. Since you are here reading this book, you obviously have a hunger to expand your awareness and embrace a heart-centered life. I ask you to stay open as we dive deeper with every page. Breathe in what resonates with you, and what does not, just exhale.

There are many paths you can take that will lead you through the unknown and into your preferred reality or a higher plane of consciousness. I am here to promote self-leadership, so I encourage you to follow your own path and connect to your inner Divine guides and teachers. I am only here to remind you of what you may have forgotten—that a power lies inside of you that can enhance your relationships, create optimal health, and bring more abundance and harmony into your life. This book is to be used as a reference tool to empower you to journey through the uncharted regions of your mind and to connect to the Divine intelligence that exists in your heart.

Keep reading and stay curious.

Higher Idea #1 Give Yourself the Gift of Time

Before we go too deep, let's talk about one thing first—*Time*. How often do you say to your friends or family, "I don't have time" or "I am too busy"?

A great life also requires *time* to be created; however, we can get caught up in the idea of *I am too busy* or *I don't have time to learn something new.*

Do you believe time is speeding up or slowing down? What if you discovered that you have the power to expand or contract time? Yes, your mind is very powerful and it is your thoughts and feelings that create your experiences.

Now, you may be juggling the many responsibilities of being a parent or being in a relationship, or you may be a business owner with a very large "To-Do" list. I get it!

Our everyday stresses and responsibilities can keep us trapped in the *busyness* of life. I know there are only twenty-four hours in a day and maybe your "To-Do" list is a mile long. But what if the next time you catch yourself saying, "I am too busy" or "I don't have time," you stop everything you are doing? Just stop! Take a moment to breathe, and then ask yourself the question, "If I am the creator of my routine, when did I allow my routine to take over my life?"

Now breathe into the word *busy* and the phrase *I don't have time.* Expand your awareness to notice how these words make you feel. Do you feel constricted or do you feel expansion? The word *busy* carries the vibration of chaos and stress especially if you leave things to the last minute.

With all this *busyness,* how can you have time to nurture your mind, body, and spirit? The answer is: Only *you* can create time for yourself. If you are caught up in the vibration of *busyness,* you may have forgotten that you are the one who created your busy schedule in the first place. Your *busyness* is a learned behavior and now you can unlearn what is not working for you.

For some reason, you have allowed your Busy self to take over your life and this self can cause you to believe that if you are not busy doing,

doing, doing, everything will fall apart. Is this true? A heart-centered life is a balance of *doing (masculine energy)* and *being (feminine energy)*.

You have the power to create your day to be exactly what you want it to be. I suggest you view time from a higher perspective. See and know that time is fluid, not linear. Time constricts when your thinking is constricted. Time expands when you feel expansion of your spirit. At the core of who you are is an ageless, eternal being unbound by time.

Fifteen years ago, I stopped wearing a watch. Why? Because as long as I was time bound, I found it more challenging to live in the present moment. The more I made the choice to live in the moment, the more I experienced time expanding. I now live on Divine time (listening to my inner clock), and I know that I am always successfully engaged in the right activity and there is plenty of time for everything. There is only *now*.

Today's Higher Idea: Release your Busy self and welcome your Creative Self. You are now releasing chaos from your life. Substitute the word busy with words that resonate at a higher frequency such as *creative, active* or *full*. You can say, "I have a full day ahead of me" or "I have plenty of time for everything."

Higher Idea #2 Define What Freedom Is to You

Now that you have plenty of time to read and explore the Freedom Frequency of life, let's explore the word *freedom*. What does *freedom* mean to you? Freedom means different things to different people. Some people want to be financially free, while others want to be free from materialism. This book embraces the idea that true freedom is the opportunity to be fully who you are and create the life that lives in your heart. This includes the freedom of all mental, emotional, and physical pain.

People who are not living in the Freedom Frequency live in fear. Many individuals do not know how to handle the power of freedom; for this reason, we have so many human laws and rules. Fear creates distrust and separation, which can cause people to react to life causing harm to others, or to steal from others, or take advantage of those less fortunate. We abuse freedom by trying to control others, which we do when we experience a deep feeling of emptiness within and disconnection from life.

You gain freedom the more you live in the present moment and when you deepen into truth and allow yourself to see the bigger picture of life. You gain freedom when you stop arguing with life and surrender to *what is*, to what life *is* in the moment and not judge it as wrong, right, good or bad. Trust that what you are experiencing is a part of your soul's contract—what you agreed to come into this life to express. Everything is happening for a higher purpose. Life is about expansion and growth. Having acceptance for where you are allows for judgment to dissolve.

You are not alone. It may feel at times that your soul is chained in a dungeon and the darkness is all you see. You are not the darkness. Freedom from pain and suffering, from lack and limitation is here for you. There is a way out of the pit of life. Freedom is your inherent birthright.

Today's Higher Idea: A simple visualization that will raise your vibration instantly is to visualize yourself climbing a ladder up out of the darkness, then place your feet on solid ground and stand in the sun – the light of integration. Do you feel a shift in how you feel in your body? Your mind is where your power lie and knowing how to use your higher mind, your Divine Mind will bring you the freedom you seek.

Higher Idea #3 The Law of Vibration

More than likely you have heard about the Law of Attraction. Simply put, the Law of Attraction states that whatever you choose to think about, negative or positive, is what you will attract into your life.

The results you are experiencing in your relationships, business, health, finances etc., are a direct result of the Law of Attraction at work whether or not you are conscious of it. The Law of Attraction is always present in every choice you make. If you are not manifesting what you want, it is because your thoughts are focusing on *what is not working* instead of what you want your life to be. For example, if you want your relationship to improve, it is wise to focus on what you want your relationship to *look* and *feel* like instead of focusing on what your beloved is doing wrong. Whatever you focus on, *you get more of.*

In order to understand fully the Law of Attraction, you need to understand another universal law: the Law of Vibration. The Law of Vibration is the foundation of the Law of Attraction. The Law of Vibration, simply put, is that everything in our universe is made up of energy, energy vibrations that transmit a frequency.

In his book, *Ageless Body, Timeless Mind*, Deepak Chopra reminds us that our body appears to be composed of solid matter that can be broken down into molecules and atoms. Quantum physics tells us that every atom is more than 99.9999 percent empty space, and the subatomic particles moving at lightning speed through this space are actually bundles of vibrating energy.

Everything, including "you," is vibrating at a specific frequency. Every atom in your cells send out an electromagnetic wave, a *vibration,* and it is this vibration of your thoughts and feelings that is transmitted out into your external world, which then creates your physical experience. For example, when you are drawn to be in a relationship, you will attract someone who has the same vibrational match as your unresolved subconscious issues. This is why being in a relationship offers you the perfect opportunity for spiritual and emotional growth. You attract a mirror of you to help you clear out lower energy vibrations so you can spiral up and spread your wings.

Energy is always in a state of motion, and we have the ability to control

7

that motion through our *emotions*, which we will explore in Chapter Two. If you want the Law of Attraction to work in your favor, then become aware of your own energy *vibration*.

When you live above the line, your vibration is high and you attract what your heart desires. To live above the line, it is important to shift your beliefs. If you don't believe you have the power to manifest more love, joy, or peace in your life, then you will not have the positive emotions required to attract it. If your thoughts are vibrating in alignment with your heart's desires, then it will be easier for you to feel excited about manifesting more of what you want. If your thoughts vibrate below the line, your manifestation abilities may be lacking. When you are vibrating above the line, you manifest with ease and grace. This is where your magic lives.

Today's Higher Idea: Share with someone your understanding of the Law of Vibration and how it applies to your life.

Higher Idea #4 Live Above the Line

You may be wondering what it means to *Live Above the Line*. Since every thought, feeling, word, action or behavior vibrates at a certain frequency, that can either spiral you down toward death or up towards more life, it would be a higher idea to know and embody those that spiral you up above the line. To simplify, I created *The Freedom Frequency Chart* on the next page to show the many vibrations within each of the two core frequencies that represent the foundation of this book: The Frequency of Fear and The Frequency of Freedom.

You will see that below the horizontal line is a small list of perceived negative emotions, actions or behaviours we experience as human beings. These lower energies can make you feel very uncomfortable and can cause you to take actions you would not otherwise take because at the core of all negative emotions is FEAR. For example, fear of being judged, fear of being rejected, fear of losing control, fear of not being good enough, fear of being misunderstood, and so on.

Above the line is where you experience the higher expressions of life such as joy, abundance, and love that you, I am sure, want to experience more of. *You are meant to LIVE ABOVE THE LINE!* Unfortunately, many of us only experience brief moments of these higher energies because we have not been taught how to spiral up and fully receive these higher vibrations of life.

Both the Frequency of Freedom and the Frequency of Fear consist of electromagnetic fields of energy vibrations. You tune into this information the same way you tune into your favorite radio station. Each frequency relates to states of mind or levels of consciousness.

Living above the line is about making a conscious choice to spiral up from living in the lower realms of negative emotions and darker forces (fear) that can destroy your relationships, your business pursuits, and your life.

The Freedom Frequency Chart

Positive Emotions and Qualities that resonate in the Freedom Frequency are:

trust	commitment	oneness	caring
compassion	bliss	appreciation	empowered
integrity	ecstasy	health	luxury
honor	connected	divine order	ease and grace
joy	synchronicity	passion	authentic
happiness	genuine	courage	passionate
respect	wealth	knowing	romantic
admired	abundance	truth	relaxed
loyalty	wholeness	remembering	playful
peace	gratitude	calm	laughter
thoughtful	valued	strength	simplicity
growth	worthy	observer	celebration
oneness	willingness	certainty	
	union	patience	

Negative Emotions and Qualities that resonate in the Fear Frequency are:

stress	low self-esteem	anger	hate
frustration	despair	jealousy	sympathy
worry	abandonment	hope	pity
unappreciated	fatigue	pain	chaos
exhausted	empty	limitation	rage
neglected	hurt	lack	despair
self doubt	humiliated	manipulation	helplessness
loneliness	confused	deception	greed
depression	discouraged	needy	depression
anxiety	sabotaged	desperate love	struggle
racism	uncertainty	guilt	disappointed
suffering	resentment	ashamed	annoyed

Figure 1

We have been living in a world of polarity, a world of opposites, negative and positive, hot and cold, dark and light, fear and love.

As human beings evolve, we transition out of this world of polarity, third dimensional living, and into higher dimensional experiences. The illusion of separation begins to dissolve and we once again come into alignment with the one truth — that we are all *one*.

You are being called to step into a grander vision of who you are, to awaken to the multi-dimensional aspects of intelligence within and then align with the highest version of who you are – your Brilliant Self.

Living above the line will change how you view your emotions, how you view your relationships, how you view yourself and your life. Your perceptions of reality will shift in very profound ways as you awaken to a reality that is much bigger than you've ever imagined.

Unfortunately, many people find the journey to freedom too uncomfortable so they make the choice to stay locked up in the predictable patterns of avoidance and live by default. I know because I lived in default for most of my life. I was unaware of my power within or how my negative thoughts and feelings created all the pain, low self-esteem, and lack of love and freedom in my life. And I was completely unaware of how I had allowed fear to control my life. Having a direct experience of *enlightened love* woke me up to the truth of reality and making the commitment to live my spirituality has been one of the biggest gifts I have ever given myself.

Today's Higher Idea: Develop a daily practice of expanding your awareness of when you are vibrating below the line and how different your life would be if you lived above the line. Observe yourself without judgment.

Higher Idea #5 Vibrate in the Freedom Frequency

How frequently do you feel free? Free from negative thoughts and emotions? How frequently do you feel happiness or joy during your day?

I have defined the Freedom Frequency as a field of higher energy vibrations that consist of positive emotions or states of higher mind that we experience or want to experience more of such as peace, trust, happiness, respect, fulfillment and so on.

The Freedom Frequency is your natural state of being where you experience a higher love for yourself and life. It is here you experience compassion and bring joy to others because you feel it in your heart. It is here that ecstasy goes beyond the orgasm, as we feel the force of the Divine vibrating through every cell of our being.

Being present with where you are right here, right now, with what you *feel* and then sitting in and breathing through the energy that is alive inside of you is where your power is. It is here that you connect to your health and wealth consciousness and truly feel the greatest power in the universe ~ *Love*. This force is found in the heart center and is only activated through your willingness to connect to Source, your I AM presence. This activation will then awaken cellular memory within your entire physical body.

The core essence of the Freedom Frequency is *love*. It is a higher love, which I refer to as *enlightened love*. Enlightened love is a direct experience of the Divine. You may experience a taste of this enlightened love as you embark on your spiritual journey and the sweetness of this love becomes a driving force to experience more. When you experience this love, you will know beyond belief that there is more to life than meets the eye. You will remember you are ONE with life.

Love, in itself, vibrates at a very high frequency, and as much as you crave the experience of love, you may often hide from it. Only when you are bold enough to make the journey through the frequency of fear, the illusion of who you are not, can your physical body resonate in the *enlightened love* vibration.

If you are ready to experience more fulfilling and meaningful relationships and feel wonderful about who you are, then the journey begins with transforming yourself at a foundational level, at a vibratory level. This transformation requires relinquishing the darker forces (fear) that hold you back so you can spiral up into the lighter energies of love and freedom.

You are here on this planet to do whatever it takes to receive and embrace the energies that vibrate in the *Freedom Frequency*. These higher vibrations are not outside of you. They live within every cell of your physical body.

Today's Higher Idea: Discover what makes you *feel happy!* I recommend you get clear on what makes you feel happy naturally. Write your Freedom Frequency List of twenty-five activities you love to do or want to experience and then imagine yourself doing these things and feeling good about who you are.

Higher Idea #6 You Are Not Your Fear

I have defined the Fear Frequency as vibrations that prevent you from completely accessing the higher vibrations in the Freedom Frequency. In other words, the Fear Frequency consists of all the negative emotions, thoughts and behaviors such as blame, anger, hate, guilt, worry, anxiety, depression, and so on. This family of lower thought vibrations creates resistance, forgetfulness and can stop you from living your full potential.

Fear is associated with the *ego*, the part of you that believes you need to be protected from the illusionary saber-tooth tiger that is just around the corner. Your ego is an outdated operating system that has had eons of programming and still believes you are in constant danger. Its only objective is to keep you living in smallness, lack and limitation. Your Ego does not want you to jump outside your comfort zone, to evolve spirituality or personally. The ego has created limiting beliefs about you and your reality and when it feels threatened, it will send a signal to your brain, causing the *flight, fight, or freeze* reaction. Your ego will resist change at any cost and can cause you to remain living in fear. The *ego* is not bad or wrong; however, if you allow fear (your ego) to control you, it can paralyze your dreams, destroy your relationships, and debilitate your health.

Fear is not who you are. Fear has been a great teacher because it reminds you to move cautiously so you may embrace the fullness of every experience. You are not meant to live in the Fear Frequency. The energy of fear is usually expressed with an array of perceived negative emotions or states of mind such as anger, frustration, confusion and stress, doubt, worry and so on, because we do not understand what is happening to us. It is up to us as seekers of self-empowerment to change our idea of what fear is by readjusting our thinking. Any type of personal or spiritual growth will be uncomfortable because it means you are stepping outside your comfort zone, outside the wall of your limited beliefs and your ego will do anything to avoid feeling uncomfortable. Fear keeps you in protection mode and if you stay in this frequency your physical body will pay the price as the energy of health and wellness do not resonate here.

Today's Higher Idea: What does fear mean to you and how has it held you back in your life? Challenge yourself to step to the edge of your comfort zone. Breathe in the uncomfortable energy. Just breathe.

Higher Idea #7 You Are the Creator of Your Life

What if you discovered that YOU are more powerful than the physical world? What if you discovered that you have an internal universe that is much more powerful than anything outside of you? If this is true, do you think it would be a higher idea to get to know how the power within you works?

You are the creator of your own reality. How? By what you choose to *think* and *feel*. Yes, your thoughts and emotions, whether positive or negative, create your reality. This is how powerful you are. You are creating your reality in the same way other people are creating theirs. Yes, every event, situation, or experience you have had, whether good, bad, ugly, or joyful, was created to assist you in wakening up to your true power.

It took me a long time to integrate this truth; the truth that I create my experiences by what I choose to believe, think and feel. In fact, the concept created a huge amount of resistance because my *ego* wanted to keep me in victim mode. After all, how could I have created all the bad stuff that has happened to me? Other people are to blame, right? Should they not be responsible for all the bad things that have happened to me? I was to discover the answer was simply, "No!" This meant I could no longer blame anyone for my negative emotions. I could no longer blame the government, God, my parents, my past boyfriends, or anyone for how I was feeling in the moment. Really? Yes! And I could no longer blame myself. When I embraced this truth, I began to resonate with the words *personal accountability*.

Personal accountability is being fully responsible for your thoughts, words, actions and experiences without blame, shame or guilt. You see everything as a process of self discovery and remembering your truth.

Your mind projects the hologram of your experience through the mental images that are emotionally charged. This is why it is so important to become aware of your thoughts and feelings and which frequency you are transmitting from—*fear or freedom*? Of course, you are not able to become aware of every thought; after all, you have approximately 70,000 thoughts a day. All you are asked to do is become aware of the thoughts that disempower you or the unkind and unloving thoughts you have about yourself or others and begin at once to exchange these lower ideas into new empowered truths. As you do, you start the process of shifting from your fear-based mind and align with your Divine Mind.

Eastern philosophy reminds us that we live in a thought-powered and feeling centered universe, which means that whatever thoughts you have that are emotionally charged you will eventually manifest in your life. Thoughts that are emotionally charged from below the line (negatively charged) are fragmented and will create stress, worry, frustration, and may make you wonder why you are having a bad day. Thoughts that resonate from above the line (positively charged) are centered in truth and will create more of the joy, inner peace, and love you may be seeking.

You are being called to rise up out of the illusory worlds of pain and suffering into worlds of love and freedom. How? By acknowledging and releasing *everything* that is in your way of creating a beautiful life.

You can get stuck in your day-to-day dramas and think that your present situation is all there is to life; however, there is much more to this reality than meets the eye. This universe is highly intelligent and filled with infinite energy that you are breathing in every second. It is not just air you breathe, it is life-force energy that is forever expanding, renewing, transforming and creating.

Begin today to see yourself as a Creator of your own life. If you are unhappy, begin projecting out a new hologram of mental images that make you feel happy. See every day as a new day to begin again. Focus on creating this day to teach you more about yourself. When your thoughts are vibrating at higher frequencies, you spiral up into greater experiences of life. Creating a solid foundation in the *Freedom Frequency* requires you to expand your awareness of who you are – the Creator of your life.

Today's Higher Idea: Creators know the universe is always expressing through them. What is ready to be expressed through you? What would you share with the world? What changes would you make?

Higher Idea #8 Choose Where You Want to Vibrate

One of the most powerful questions you can ask yourself every day is, "Where am I vibrating right now, *fear* or *freedom*?"

The emotions or states of mind in The *Freedom Frequency* Chart (Higher Idea #4) are ones to which we can all relate. There are many more positive or perceived negative emotions or qualities available than the ones I listed. This chart is to be used as a reference for the emotionally charged vibrations you may experience throughout your life.

Each positive or perceived negative emotion or state defines a rate of vibration, a level of consciousness that determines how you will think and behave. If you are interested in knowing the exact rate of vibrations, I suggest Dr. David R. Hawkins' book, *Power vs. Force.* Hawkins developed a map of the different levels of consciousness, otherwise known as the Emotional Scale. Shame, for example, vibrates at a frequency of 20, which is the lowest on the scale, while enlightenment is the highest at 700+.

Many of us move in and out of various vibrations and in doing so, we experience the contrasts of reality. We are all here to experience the lower vibrations contained in the Fear Frequency; however, we are not meant to live here. We are meant to spiral up, to evolve, and to embody the higher vibrations experienced in the Freedom Frequency. This doesn't mean you are to ignore or suppress your negative emotions. In fact, the only way to spiral up is to *feel* everything that is ALIVE inside of you, all *emotions* without making it wrong, right, good, or bad. I will share powerful practices in the following chapters.

We have all experienced the emotional roller-coaster of pain or pleasure. Our earthly experience allows us to explore all of the energy available to us. Many of us move up and down the scale from the low-energy fields of separation and lack, and then we move up to experience the high-energy fields of joy and alignment with our soul within the frequency of freedom. What many of us discover is that we do not know how to handle the high-energy vibrations contained in the Freedom Frequency for an extended period of time because we are uncomfortable with the intensity and the power it brings.

Do you remember a moment when you were blissfully happy and then a

17

voice within said, "I wonder how long this will last?" With that doubting thought you spiral down once more, riding the roller-coaster into the frequency of fear. How long do you stay here? Until you take back your power and remember the *light* within. You stay in this lower vibration until you learn recognize the gift of your present experience.

The greatest illusion many people hold is the illusion that the physical world is more powerful than they are. As I mentioned earlier, one of the biggest secrets is that your internal universe (emotional, mental and spiritual) is much more powerful than anything outside of you. It is a higher idea to begin now and turn your attention inward and explore this inner universe. Let go of allowing the media or outside forces to dictate what you should believe, or think.

The key to living above the line is Self Awareness. Becoming self aware is observing where your thoughts and emotions take you. Self awareness leads to being Self-Directive, directing yourself to live and experience the highest version of you. Learning to direct your thoughts and emotions is realized by observing the fear-based energy and love-based energy that is moving through you without judging it as good or bad. Becoming an observer of yourself, of your personality or the voices in your head and not taking it all personally, leads to one direction – unity consciousness.

There is a powerful technique I created called, the *Divine Mind Conversation* (Chapter Seven), where you learn how to be in the energy of your Divine Mind, the unified field of intelligence and unify all fear-based energy with Enlightened Love energy. In other words, you are bringing your ego and soul into divine union. When the idea of separation or the power struggle in your mind is dissolved, you are on your way to becoming whole and complete as a human being.

Through the process of education and expanding *self-awareness*, you can gain the knowledge and insights to uplift your life. As your awareness expands and your inner worlds awaken, you begin to embrace the realm of *remembering* who you are.

Today's Higher Idea: One of the most powerful questions you can ask yourself is, "Where am I vibrating right now, *fear* or *freedom*?" You are the only one who can consciously choose which frequency you will live in.

Higher Idea #9 Get Real with Where You Are

In order to spiral up in life and live above the line, you will be required to get real with where you are right now. Get real with where you are financially, in your relationships, your environment, your health, your spirituality, your family, and how you feel about your career. This means defining for yourself what you want, what you need, what you believe in, what is important to you and what your heart desires. In order to know where you want to go in life, you first need to know where you're at.

Facing reality will feel uncomfortable. Why? Because for the most part we do not like looking at ourselves. For instance, some people would rather avoid opening their bills because they fear they won't have enough money to pay them, or married couples will sleep with their children to avoid intimacy with a spouse, or people will avoid a daily meditation practice because they fear their own light.

The more you face and admit to what is present in your life, the more clarity you have around what is working and what is not. Only then can you say, "I have had enough of living this way." Nobody can do this for you. Stop waiting. You are not a follower. You are a leader of your own life. Yes, you will feel uncomfortable as you experience the energy of vulnerability; however, I do not know of any empowered or enlightened human beings who did not move through the *uncomfortableness*, the energy of fear, or intense resistance to become who they are today.

Confusion, chaos, and stress lessen dramatically when you get real with where you are at and face the truth of what *is*. Now, the energy of clarity, focus, direction, and soul-inspired action can spiral you up into living the life your heart desires. You are meant to be happy.

Happiness is realized when you ground yourself in truth, in your own spirituality. A truth that can shift your life in very profound ways is remembering that nothing in this world is solid or unchanging because your thoughts and emotions are made of energy and energy is constantly moving. For example, you may be angry with your partner because you feel he/she does not listen to your request for more respect and therefore you avoid him/her. However; if you both sat down and expressed in a healthy way, about how this experience reminds you of when you were a child and no one listened to you, you pop the bubble of blame and projections.

This truth releases so much pent up negative emotions that have been suppressed and allows for a healing to take place and your vibration to shift dramatically.

Topics that cause you to feel vulnerable are the exact topics you need to be having conversations about. When you admit and acknowledge your dissatisfaction with your present experience, not from a place of continuously complaint or blame, but facing the truth in how you *feel*, you allow the negative energetic charge you have around your experience to be released.

All the uncomfortable or painful feelings you have about life's issues can eventually transform into curiosity and interest. You are that powerful. Your thoughts and emotions are constantly changing. You can feel depression one moment and enlightenment in the next.

Get real with *what is;* then accept *what is,* and allow life to unfold naturally. The universe knows what you need to heal and will create scenarios for this to occur. As you say "Yes" to facing each moment, becoming present with your thoughts and feelings, and expressing your truth, your life will start to shift and spiral up.

Creating your personal foundation involves knowing what you believe in, what you stand for, what is important to you, or what you value the most. If you want to experience freedom, you will be asked to step into and acknowledge your present reality.

Today's Higher Idea: Let today be your starting point. Take a moment and write where you're at in your relationship, your career, your finances, your family, and your health. Write about what you do not like and what you will no longer tolerate. You are where you are because of the choices you have made. Now clarify what you want to experience in each life area. Do not edit your thoughts. Write! Write! Write!

Higher Idea #10 Shift Your Perception

The reality you experience is perceptual, meaning everything is based on how you interpret life events. Your view of life depends greatly upon the experiences you have growing up, which then create beliefs about who you think you are.

As you mature, your perceptions—how you view yourself, others, and your life—dictates what you will experience. For example, if you are a woman and perceive men as emotionally unavailable, then that is what you will experience. If you are a man and you view women as gold diggers, than you will attract those kind of women. If you believe the world is ending then you will draw others with similar beliefs to your story. If you perceive the world you live in as unsafe or dangerous, then you will not feel safe or supported, no matter what you do. If your perception of your mother or father is negative, then your experience with your mother or father will not be pleasant.

Some people have experienced so much pain that they choose to live a life with walls around their hearts and minds. What they do not realize is that the emotional and mental pain they hold on to can be transformed and released by shifting their perceptions of their past experiences.

The vibration of feeling disconnected to life, having a lack of energy, or feeling overwhelmed can be easily changed by simply shifting your perception. Life involves the journey of letting go, the *letting go* of old stories and limited belief structures from eons of programming can be challenging. It probably took people a while to adjust to the new perception that the world was no longer flat.

Perceiving your reality from a spiritual perspective brings incredible freedom. For example, if you feel unloved or unappreciated, turn the other way towards the world out there. Look around you and see if there is a *soul* that needs your help. Maybe you have been divinely called to be at this place in time for a higher purpose? To selflessly serve someone. As you seek higher perspectives, you are shown the next step on your path to greater fulfillment.

Today's Higher Idea: If you were to sit on a cloud and view your life from above, from a higher vantage point, what changes would you make in how you behave with others? A shift in perception goes a long way.

Higher Idea #11 Benefits of Raising Your Vibration

As human beings, we are motivated in one of two ways. We are either moving away from pain or moving toward pleasure. Every day, we are being sold a product or a service that will help us escape the pain of life or create more pleasure in our lives. The motivation to buy anything comes from knowing how it will benefit our lives.

One of the greatest benefits of raising your vibration from a fear-based consciousness to a love-based consciousness is that you will never feel *lonely* again. Guaranteed! When the energy in your body is vibrating in freedom, you will automatically feel connected to all of life, to the Source of All That Is.

I discovered for myself, when my energy vibration was above the line in the Freedom Frequency, illness became less frequent. The vibration of health is your natural state and here your body *flows* energy with ease.

Another amazing benefit is that you will never have to go looking for love ever again! That's right! It is all right here now! As you awaken to the Divine love that lives in every cell of your physical body, and consciously expand this vibration out through your heart, you become an attraction magnet drawing people, resources, and whatever you desire into your reality.

Raising your energy vibration will bring the joy, the love, and all the delicious qualities of life into your field of experience. If you do not know how to shift your vibration, keep reading. It is obvious that you are open, willing, and a ready student. This willingness to learn and know the truth about the power that lies inside of you is benefiting your life right now.

Raising your vibration you will know that you are always safe. If you don't feel safe, you lack trust. Trust must be cultivated from within in order to spiral up. As you raise your vibration you begin to trust in yourself as you have the inner knowing that the journey you are on is divinely perfect. When you project out the vibration of love and gratitude to the earth and all of humanity, life will support you, Mother Earth will support you and people you have never met will support you.

If you feel uncertain about what steps to take, this book is intended to remind you to spiral up through your fear, your doubt, your pain, and into a higher love and acceptance for who you are. When you are feeling vulnerable, this is a sign that you are on the right track.

As you raise your vibration, you enter higher states of consciousness, which means you are rising above the fear that consumes many. Living above the line, you embody the higher vibrations of life and will no longer be affected by the negative behaviors or reactions of others. You will see that the only reason people behave negatively is because they are in fear.

The purpose of this journey on earth is for you to remember who you are and to discover that you are much more than what your physical eyes can see. As you spiral up and lighten up your energy vibration and have a more positive outlook on life, you will begin to see more than what you do now. You will have more energy to do what you need to do. You will look and feel younger, without the aid of drugs or surgery because you are living in the present moment. You will feel a sense of peace within your mind where nothing really bothers you anymore. You will be more accepting of others and who you are. Everything that used to affect you in a negative way no longer will. You will feel a stronger connection with your family and oneness with the world. You will create things and do things you never thought you could before. And the only food, drink or clothes, you will want *in* or *on* your body is high quality. The higher you vibrate the more you raise your standards and your *deservability* factor.

As you raise your energetic vibration from being negatively charged to positively charged, you realize that all the negative thoughts and voices in your head have vanished. You now have one voice, the voice of wisdom, the voice of your Brilliant Self who guides you through life's moments with ease and grace.

There are so many more incredible benefits when you raise your vibration including being happy for no reason.

Today's Higher Idea: Shifting your vibration means that life, as you know it, will change. Any time you feel confused, want to give up, or are frustrated about the journey you are on, remember the benefits of shifting your vibration.

Higher Idea #12 You Always Have a Choice

You have a choice in what you choose to focus on, what you choose to express, and the life you choose to create. You have a choice to think negatively or positively about your life experiences. You have a choice either to say, "Yes" or "No." Your life is made up of choices, and if you do not like what you are creating, then it may be time to make a different choice.

One thing is certain: Life will always throw issues, problems, or challenges your way because that is how you discover what you're made of and who you are. The trick is in knowing how to deal with life's challenges and how to overcome fear. You now have a choice to begin viewing all challenges as opportunities to learn about yourself.

You also have the choice to think different thoughts about the people in your life. You can choose to see them as divine messengers who are only in your life to remind you of how you see yourself. By making healthier choices based on your values, you lift your life up and attract people of value. You can gain a better understanding of where you are in life by recognizing what frequency zone you are working from—*fear* or *freedom?*

Expanding your awareness of the power that lives inside of you offers you a choice to learn from love instead of riding the roller-coaster into the lower vibrations of chaos, struggle, and suffering to learn your life lessons. This does not mean the chaos will end. If the seed of chaos no longer lives inside of you, then the chaos created by others will simply become scenery on your ride to living above the line.

Moving out of the *fear frequency* is about *light*ening up! You can choose the feeling of freedom anytime by anchoring lighter energies of love, joy, trust, and understanding into your thoughts on a continuous basis. You also have a choice to let go of eating heavy, processed, fear-injected food and spiral up into eating food that carries life-force energy (*light*) such as fruits and vegetables.

Today's Higher Idea: Demand more from yourself and say, "I choose to feel happiness today." "I choose to make someone smile today." "I choose to say, 'I love you', and 'I'm sorry'."

Higher Idea #13 Commitment Request

Only when you are committed to a higher vision or a higher idea of who you are and what you want your life to be, can the universe work its magic. Make your commitment to evolve because you see the intelligence behind it.

State the following out loud:

- I now commit to being flexible and accepting change as a part of life.
- I now commit to discovering the truth of who I am.
- I ask for my soul to activate and my heart to open.
- I now relinquish all lower thoughts and ideas that do not serve me.
- I now breathe in the gift of trust and acceptance.
- I now relinquish all fear that limits me.
- I now choose to remember my own value.
- I now commit to understanding my reality and my purpose in it.
- I ask that I experience life with ease and grace.
- I now commit to remembering my Divine perfection, my greatness, my beauty, and my truth.
- I commit to deepening my spiritual practice and living in truth.
- I am now committed to reading The *Freedom Frequency* from front to back and completing every exercise, as it will benefit my life.

    So it is!

Chapter Two
Emotional Evolution

Humanity is experiencing an emotional evolution. I define emotional evolution as having a higher level of awareness that we are only responsible for how we feel and we are not responsible for how others feel. We are now embracing higher ideas and becoming personally accountable for the energy that moves through us. We are ending the blame game.

In this chapter, we will explore your emotions as an intelligent energy that is alive inside of you. I will offer you a powerful new way to view your emotions and how they can serve you. For instance, what if you could view your emotions from a higher perspective? How? By viewing the energy that is alive inside of you from a place of neutrality, by becoming a witness or observer of the fluid energy that moves through you.

When you shift into observer mode you take your power back because you are no longer personalizing your emotions. This doesn't mean ignoring how you feel, in fact, you will embrace how you feel more than ever. As you spiral up in higher states of consciousness, the polarity of good and bad, negative and positive begins to dissolve, and you then become an observer of the energy vibrations that flow through you.

Exploring and learning how to work with your emotional dimension will have a powerful and positive impact on all your relationships and life experience. The inner work involved may be challenging, time-consuming, and require great patience, but the rewards are worth it.

Higher Idea #14 Emotional Integrity

Do you believe that emotions represent weakness? Do you do whatever it takes to hide the heavy burden you are carrying? Do you hide behind drugs, alcohol, sex, food, or your career so you won't have to *feel*? Will you do anything to escape *feeling*? The incredible thing about life is that it always forces us to change our limited ideas, and if we continue to ignore the natural laws of creation, the cycle of destruction, tragedy, or death is sure to remind us.

Many people have lost their employment, relationships, or connections with family or friends because they don't know how to deal with their emotions. Others stay emotionally distant because they have difficulty managing the complexity of feelings, decisions, and conflicting energies. If we want to improve the quality of our life, knowing how to work with our emotional dimension will assist in building self-esteem and the confidence to handle any situation, be it personal or professional. We no longer need to buy into the fear and doubt that once paralyzed us.

Emotional Integrity is the personal achievement of having control of your emotions, and at the same time, acknowledging your emotions when they rise up. Emotional Integrity involves accountability, inner strength, and discipline of thoughts. The benefit of Emotional Integrity is that you will no longer be affected in a negative way by what people say or do.

Emotional Integrity is the ability to recognize the truth behind your feelings. If you are unable to manifest what you want in life, it's because you have yet to clear out fear-based energies (limiting beliefs) from your subconscious mind.

You can rise above your pain when you discover the *seed* of your emotions and explore the truth of what you are feeling. You have the power to release heavy energies trapped in your physical body and exchange them for lighter energies that can spiral you up to live above the line. This does not mean creating an emotional scene in order to get your way or to manipulate someone. This pattern will only give you more of what you *don't* want. You are here to release your *fear* of the energy that moves through you.

Every human being has both masculine and feminine energies moving through his or her physical body. Our masculine qualities represent the leader within, the one who is action-orientated, strategizes, and protects while our feminine qualities mirror that of the nurturer, receiver, and flow of emotions. Allowing these energies to be expressed in a balanced and healthy way is essential to our spiritual and emotional evolution.

An extreme shift within men and women has taken place over the last two decades; women, who were once extremely emotional, have now shut down their feeling centers in order to operate in the masculine world of power, control, and action. Women are being guided now to embrace their Divine feminine and dissolve the closed or guarded hearts they have toward men or the masculine energy within. Thankfully, more men are experiencing a transformation as they embrace their feminine energies within. Where emotions were once avoided, men are now giving themselves permission to feel and allow tears to flow dissolving past myths of what courage and strength really mean.

It is only a guarded or closed heart that stops us from experiencing the depth of our own feelings. As women and men embrace a more heart-centered life together, we harmonize the energies of masculine and feminine and have the power to create heaven on earth.

Today's Higher Idea: Free yourself from the idea that emotions are weak and allow for a deeper expression to be realized. Talk to someone you trust about how you feel or take time to write in your journal and express your truth.

Higher Idea #15 Discover Your Guidance System

Do you know the number one cause of a ruined vacation or what has the power to ruin a special evening, end a relationship, or a business opportunity? The answer is *destructive negative emotions.*

Since our third dimension is based in polarity, at opposite ends of the spectrum, we experience two main frequencies *fear* and *love (freedom)* and everything in between. One is based in illusion and the other in truth. All emotions, positive and negative, vibrate within the range of these two main frequencies.

From this point forward, I recommend you view your emotions as your internal guidance system. If you are feeling uncomfortable in your skin, it means your thoughts are incorrect and you are vibrating in the Fear Frequency. If you are feeling happy about yourself and your life, it means your thoughts are in alignment with truth and you are vibrating in the Freedom Frequency. For example, if you are feeling stressed (below the line), your body is telling you to stop what you are doing and find a quiet place to meditate so you can shift your vibration. When you are stressed, your mind is in overwhelm and cannot come up with a solution. You will benefit greatly the more you tune in and listen to your body. Yoga is another powerful gift you can give yourself as it will reduce the tension build up and you will learn how to ground and *be* in your body.

Emotion is *energy in motion,* and this energy flows through every cell of your physical body. Listening to your inner guidance system means tuning into how you feel in your body in the present moment. How you feel either represents the vibration of *ease* (above the line) or the vibration of *dis-ease* (below the line). If the energy in your body is negatively charged (not in ease), then you are being reminded to stop what you are doing, meditate, and contemplate a different course of action that speaks to your heart.

Today's Higher Idea: Your fear-based emotions are like red flags warning you about the thoughts you are having. Practice non-judgment of these emotions when they arise. Could your thoughts or perceptions be incorrect about the situation? Where is your mind directing you – *fear or freedom?* Get *real* with how you *feel* so you can let it pass. You are here to *flow* the lower energies through you not become it.

29

Higher Idea #16 See Your Emotions as Liquid Energy

Emotions are the same for everyone. Throughout our lives we all experience the roller-coaster of perceived positive and negative emotions. The only difference from one person to the next is the degree to which we allow perceived negative emotions to take us down into the lower realms of fear and consume our lives.

Are you willing to connect to your Courageous Self and explore the depths of your subconscious, which is the feeling center of your being? In order to progress mentally, emotionally, spiritually, and physically, you will be required to acknowledge and be present with any fear-based energy that has been holding you back. We will explore the other phases of mind in Chapter Three, because it is the invisible aspects of who you are, that holds the key to lasting transformation.

Your mind can become attached to people, ideas, things, or events, and it is your emotional attachments and how you interact with other people that create the emotional roller-coaster you often experience. Since life is about beginnings and endings or creation and destruction, everyone eventually experiences detachment or loss. You may experience the end of an intimate relationship, death of a loved one, or loss of a job, which can create the feeling of being rejected, unloved, or unsupported.

Your emotional dimension connects you to stored memories in your subconscious mind and the uncomfortable truths attached to unresolved issues. Emotions, positive or negative, create long-term memories, which become locked up in your cells. Depending on whether you have installed pleasant or unpleasant memories within your cells determines how you will perceive the many moments that make up your life. Emotional integrity involves the process of filtering out and transforming the collective lower thought forms (beliefs) from your subconscious mind so you can free yourself from painful memories or your wounded stories and live fully in the present moment.

It's time to take a closer look at the lower energies that move through your body and how you can learn to control them so your life integrates with the higher vibrations in the Freedom Frequency.

Viewing your emotions as energy flowing through you like water, allows you to step out of *becoming* your negative emotions. This distinction will change your life and shift how you relate to others in very profound ways. Again, it is important to emphasize here that you will require a certain amount of inner strength to readjust your thinking.

Since you have a desire to live above the line, then all family, financial, self-related, or sexual issues that hold a negative emotional charge will require your attention. This means that every time you are triggered or your buttons are pushed (congratulate the person who has the power to do this as they are divinely here to assist you in achieving emotional maturity) you are being asked to get real with how you feel.

A negative emotional charge with others only leads to lost or missed opportunities that could have brought many gifts. This is why it is important to bring your emotional energy into harmonic balance, and once your negative interactions with others become neutralized, you have become an empowered human being.

Your emotions are constantly changing from one moment to the next. For instance, you can go from a state of sadness and within moments be laughing at your predicament. In one moment you can be angry with your spouse and the next minute your heart is open to love. You connect to your inner power the more you begin to see your emotions as fluid, energy flowing through you and constantly changing. You have the power to feel what you want to feel in every moment.

Greg Braden is a thought leader, bestselling author, speaker and a brilliant teacher of spiritual science. Through his work I have learned so much about myself. A powerful quote I found by this wise man is:

Modern science has discovered that through each emotion we experience in our bodies, we also undergo chemical changes of things such as pH and hormones that mirror our feelings. Through the "positive" experiences of love, compassion, and forgiveness and the "negative" emotions of hate, judgment, and jealousy, we each possess the power to affirm or deny our existence at each moment of every day.

~ Greg Braden

Today's Higher Idea: From the *Freedom Frequency* List in Higher Idea #4, express out loud which states of being, you are ready to claim such as, "I AM joy! I AM peace! I AM love!" Claim it! Louder!

Higher Idea #17 See the Gift of Negative Emotions

Viewing my perceived negative emotions as a gift transformed my life completely. Growing up, I used to be so frustrated with my parents and their inability to communicate with one another. Their negative interactions and emotional way of being were transferred to me, and I carried their beliefs like a monkey on my back right into my adult life. When I was bored in my relationships, I would stir the pot and create drama by yelling and venting as I had no idea what to do with all the uncomfortable energy inside my body. I played the blame game just like my parents had.

Yes, I wore the face of a happy person when I was out in the world, but in my home, I became a wild woman and had many moments of rage especially toward the men in my life. Underneath the anger stirred a deep sadness and underneath the sadness were many layers of fear such as the fear of being misunderstood, fear of abandonment, fear of being unloved, and the fear of rejection. Of course, I was completely unaware that my negative emotions were based in fear; in fact, if you had told me I was living in fear, I would have thought you were a crazy person. I was ignorant because I lacked the knowledge and understanding of myself, my emotions, and the truth of my reality.

We are not given a life manual in school or taught how to handle the intense emotional energy that moves through us. I am grateful to have been downloaded a path of internal freedom from spirit many years ago as I was shown how I was to live my life and then how I could guide others to follow their own heart. It was not an easy journey at first as my fear-based mind did not want to let go. After all, it had been with me for so long.

As I awakened spiritually and deepened into my practice of daily meditation, I began to see the many invisible and multi-dimensional worlds that made up my life experience. I discovered that changing my perceptions about my emotions was a huge gift in itself.

You have the power to transform the seed of all negative emotions; however, these emotions can only be transformed authentically when you are open to receiving the gift each one brings to your life.

A gift you can give yourself is to remember that you are not your emotions. Emotions are a form of intelligence wanting to be experienced by you. You are not meant to become and be overtaken by emotions. You can only *feel* anger. You can only feel jealousy. You can only *feel* sadness. Once you *feel* the emotion fully, which means acknowledging, and embracing the energy, you then release it by allowing it to flow through. How? Keep reading.

All perceived negative emotions remind you that there is something in your life that requires your attention and needs to be resolved. Underneath anger is sadness, and underneath sadness is fear. Therefore, we need to get real with ourselves and acknowledge the fear within. Underneath your fear is a power so great - *your Divine Mind.*

Many people have a difficult time believing they fear anything at all; however, all perceived negative emotions are associated with one or many fears such as fear of being misunderstood, fear of being wrong, fear of losing control, being alone, not being heard, and so on. Anger, for example, is an obvious reflection of deep dissatisfaction with our life and a desperate yearning for change.

To make this simple, let's imagine a cherry pie that is filled with one hundred cherries. Each cherry represents an emotion, some being positive and some being negative (experience duality then unity). The totality of who you are is the complete cherry pie. Now, all the positively charged cherries are sweet and yummy and all the negatively charged cherries are sour and poisonous. Your role on earth is to transform all your sour and poisonous cherries into sweet and delicious cherries so you become a Divine cherry pie that attracts everyone who is vibrating in positive resonance. Each human being is expressing from a place of either Divine sweetness or poisonous ego. Not good or bad. It just *IS.*

From this point forward, see yourself having "Emotional Moments". Not stressful days, or angry weeks or depressing years. Moments!

Today's Higher Idea: If you look at the Freedom Frequency Chart (Higher Idea #4) and add up all the fear-based energies you experience, then you know how many sour and poisonous cherries you are ready to transform into sweet and yummy cherries. What gifts are you willing to see behind any perceived negative emotions you have experienced in the last month?

Higher Idea #18 Only Your Thoughts Make You Feel

At the beginning of this chapter I stated that humanity is experiencing an emotional evolution. I defined emotional evolution as *having a higher level of awareness that we are only responsible for how we feel and we are not responsible for how others feel.*

What did you feel about this statement? Any resistance? Let me clarify. Here is the biggest secret of all. You may want to sit down for this one. Okay, here it is…Nothing outside of you can make you angry, frustrated, happy, or sad. I know this concept may be difficult to grasp, and you may resist the idea at first, but the truth is, no one makes you feel *angry,* no one makes you feel *sad,* and no one has the power to make you feel happy. No one has the power to make you feel *anything.* It is only your *thoughts* that have that power to make you *feel.* Take a deep breath into your belly and exhale slowly.

Remember, you are the creator of your life experience. This means you can no longer blame anyone or anything outside of yourself for any of your life experiences. Your *soul* made a contract to come to this planet to awaken and remember the *love* that it is. If you needed to experience drama, trauma or tragedy to awaken your heart to love yourself, then all is divinely perfect. You are on a journey of remembering. Yes, this is personal accountability or should I say, *soul accountability.*

When you acknowledge the source of your emotions and realize that how you feel in the moment has nothing to do with anyone outside of yourself, you will be empowered. It is only your thoughts, your beliefs, and the mental image you have *within* you that create your emotions and perceptions of reality. Nothing outside of you is the cause.

As human beings we have always been resistant to new ideas. Take time to allow this information, this *trans-formation,* to integrate into every cell of your body. You are being called to live and be fully accountable for everything in your life, including how you *feel.*

Today's Higher Idea: Say to yourself, "I am now personally accountable for how I feel." Now instead of saying, "I am angry," you can say, "I feel angry." Instead of saying, "I am frustrated," you can say, "I am feeling frustrated." Or better yet, "I am feeling fear and letting it pass through me as I AM remembering that I AM LOVE."

Higher Idea #19 You Are Not a Victim of Life

Do you have a *Poor Me* story? If you do, it will stop you from raising your vibration and living above the line. Self-pity is a very destructive emotion that will trap you in lower life experiences. People use self-pity as an excuse to be victims. Excuses such as, "He made me do it," or "She makes me so angry" are victim talk. The Poor Me self misinterprets life's events as being wrong or bad instead of seeing everything as a learning opportunity to remember Self Love and Enlightened Love for others.

If you let the feeling of being sorry for yourself consume you, you will create more of what you do not want. This is when you need to discipline the fear-based mind and give space to the Empowered Self that says, "I have had enough! I am now going to move into action and bring more of what I want into my life."

If you have ever wondered why you have negative or manipulating people in your life, it is because a deeper part of you resonates with that person. We only associate and bond with people we resonate with— *those who vibrate at the same frequency as we do.* For instance, if you are vibrating in the Fear Frequency, you may feel the emotions of anger, blame, resentment, neglect, abuse or betrayal. If your thoughts choose to remain bitter, yet you seek relationships, you will only attract others who mirror your unresolved issues.

Victim consciousness is where people blame others for how they feel. If one stays in the victim vibe for too long, he or she will eventually attract those with a predator consciousness. Why? Because victims and predators vibrate at the same level of consciousness, just like the abused and the abuser. I know because I have been raped and abused. The only way I was going to attract respectful men into my life was first to start respecting and loving myself and to see my body as the temple that housed my soul. Secondly, I had to make the choice to no longer tolerate such behavior from anyone. Then I had to change the mental images I carried in my mind because men could only show up in my life with what I believed to be true. I had to change the way I viewed men and see that not all men were unkind or uncaring. I chose to believe that I could and would attract only loving, respectful, and kind men into my life, authentic *gentlemen*. Once I made the choice to connect with the higher energies that live above the line, I spiraled up and began to attract people in my life who respected, honored, and supported my journey.

If you are transmitting desperate or needy energy signals they are read loud and clear in any environment where you play or work. It is here that you can allow for clarity and ask yourself, "Am I playing the role of a victim?" If you are, give yourself the gift of time to reflect on your invisible dimensions (emotional, spiritual, and mental) to help you shift your beliefs and patterns. The neediness is a reflection of a lack of love for self, a lack of self-love. When you stop feeling sorry for yourself and end the game of trying to please others in order to be liked, and begin to see that everything has happened to you for a higher purpose you will begin to spiral up. Everything in life is designed to take you in one direction, to waking you up and remembering who you are. You are not a victim of life. You are extraordinary beyond belief.

It is also important to release the idea that you need to feel sorry for others. Let go of the idea that you need to pity others. Each human being is on his or her own journey, and only that person's soul knows what lessons she or he needs to learn. We cannot judge other people's choices as wrong, right, good, or bad. It is all perfectly orchestrated, and we are not here to interfere. We can give guidance and send our love, but we need to allow others to make their own choices and respect those choices no matter how we might feel.

The Pity self is also one who complains, and a complainer is always dissatisfied with life; that's fear-based living. I recommend you make the choice never to complain again and instead to breathe in the energy of gratitude. Gratitude will spiral you up faster than you can say, *"freedom frequency"*.

Today's Higher Idea: Discipline yourself to stop complaining or blaming others for one week, then two and then keep going. Instead of focusing on the negative behaviors or attitudes of others, focus on adjusting your own thoughts and actions. What can you do to add joy and comfort to those around you? Remember, complaining resonates below the line.

Higher Idea #20 Meet Your Inner Fallen Angels

Have you ever wondered where the voices you hear in your head come from? What if you discovered that for every perceived negative/positive emotion or quality you experience, there is an *Internal Self* that belongs to that voice? Since emotion is energy and energy is divinely intelligent, it would make sense that this intelligence has a voice.

From a spiritual perspective, I see every human being as an Earth Angel here to collectively co-create heaven on earth. When I refer to heaven, I am not referring to the heaven in the religious sense as something out there with a bearded man in the clouds. I am referring to an earthly experience where we, as human beings, have all opened our eyes to the truth, the truth that love, peace, beauty, joy, and abundance is here for every soul to experience fully. You are here to create a beautiful life.

Birthing onto this planet, you are born innocent and connected to the whole. As you grew up you forgot where you came from, allowing the lower energies of third dimensional life to lull you to sleep. This physical world was created so you could experience yourself as separate from the whole and then make the journey to remembering who you truly are—an *Earth Angel* of love and light. When you see beyond the veils of illusion, you will see that heaven is right here, right now.

If you stay in darkness (forgetfulness) too long, your soul becomes fragmented and each fragmented part becomes attached to negative experiences of your past life, thus creating the negative voices you hear in your mind or the constant negative thoughts rising up from the depths of your subconscious mind. It sounds like I am talking about schizophrenia and maybe we all are to some degree. Controlling our mind and emotions can be challenging especially if you've ever raged at someone or lost your mind for a moment. Then you probably wondered how you got so out of control, almost as if you were a puppet on a string. We now have to ask ourselves, "Who is holding the strings?"

You are here to free yourself and cut the strings. How? Keep reading. There are fragmented parts of ourselves that have had many labels such as gremlins, shadow selves, demons of the mind, or dark forces. These names do not create a high level of willingness for us to go in and explore ourselves, so I created the name, *Fallen Angel*. The word angel symbolizes an *angle of light* that has been blocked from reflecting truth.

When I imagine a Fallen Angel, I see an angel with a broken wing. Many of us humans have become angels with broken wings. This perspective allows us to have a deeper level of compassion for ourselves and ignite a willingness to go inward, seek out our own inner Fallen Angels and restore the love. I recommend that you let go of any religious associations of Fallen Angels (outside of you) and instead, focus and connect to your own spirituality (within you). See yourself in a whole new light.

Now, let's look at your emotions from a higher perspective. What if you saw all your perceived negative emotions as your inner Fallen Angels who live below the line and all your positive emotions as your Forgotten Angels, and they live above the line. Your journey on earth involves learning how to transform your inner Fallen and Forgotten angels into Remembered Angels so you can spread your wings and be whole and complete as a Divine human being.

Right now, let's take a moment and explore your Inner Fallen Angels and what they have to teach you. I believe there is a defining moment in our lives when these Fallen Angels take over our mind, body, and soul, just like I mentioned in the introduction happened to me when I was a teenager. Some people are aware of this moment while others are not.

Fallen Angels are the storytellers, the voices in your head that make you believe you are not worthy, that you do not deserve goodness, or that you will never manifest what you want or that you are not good enough or do not know enough. Can you relate?

Your inner Fallen Angels symbolize the fragmented *selves* of your personality and they live in the Fear Frequency. At the core of the Fear Frequency is your *ego*. The ego does not want you to connect to your Forgotten Angels who reside above the line because that is where your power lies.

Your Fallen Angels include: The Wounded self who carries the seed of all wounds, the Guilty self who carries the seed of all your guilt, the Stressful self who carries the seed of all your stresses, the Frustrated self who carries the seed of all your frustrations, the Sad self who carries the seed of all your sadness, and the Angry self who carries the seed of all your anger. And the list goes on. If you find yourself stressed, frustrated, or angry way too often, the only way to end the cycle of these negative

38

emotions is to turn inward and finally see your *selves*, the Fallen Angel within who carries the seed. In this way, you become fully accountable and can no longer blame your job, spouse, family, or outer life for how you feel. This is the true essence of *self-responsibility*—the ability to respond rather than react to the energy that is alive inside.

Your Fallen Angels will continually tell you stories to keep your vibration in the Fear Frequency so they can survive, control you, manipulate you, and deceive you into actions and behaviors that are unhealthy and do not serve your greater good. Each Fallen Angel is a multi-dimensional aspect of your mind with it own personality and its own defense system. They remain in control until you make the conscious choice to take your power back.

There are many internal *selves* among your inner Fallen Angels; however, in the next three Higher Ideas I have highlighted three Fallen Angels—the Guilty self, the Angry self, and the Addictive self, who have the ability to damage or destroy relationships and your dreams.

I created the *Divine Mind Conversation*, which is a powerful way to dissolve any and all negative energy you may have wrapped around your past experiences. Releasing the negative energetic charge you have within your mind and body is the key to raising your vibration and living in the Freedom Frequency. This is a powerful tool as you learn how to acknowledge and listen to the negative voices within and become *liberated*. Discovering what you did not know you did not know about yourself will unlock eons of programming and raise your vibration.

You will know when the negative energetic charge has been released when you are no longer triggered or react from a place of fear. You no longer take anything your Fallen Angels say, personally. The *Divine Mind Conversation* shows you how to become the observer of yourself (the many selves) and once your Fallen Angels no longer affect you in a negative way; you now open yourself up to the higher vibrations of life. Now you have the ability to ignite, embrace and illuminate your inner Forgotten Angels (your Divine power) which will profoundly transform your life.

Today's Higher Idea: Become aware of the negative voices in your head. Define which ones control you and whether you are ready to take your power back.

Higher Idea #21 Release Your Guilty Self

If you have the voice in your head that says, "I should have done this", or "I should have done that", or "I should be more…", or "I should not have done that", then you are allowing your Guilty Self to take over your life. What if you discovered that everything you have ever said or done was meant to happen for the evolutionary growth of everyone involved?

We all have an internal meter reader, which lets you know how you truly feel about the actions you are taking. Guilty pleasures are actions you believe you should not do, but you do them anyway.

Your Guilty self can drain you emotionally, and lower your self-esteem if you let it run your life. Ultimately, your Guilty self can cause regret and shame related to past events about what you believe you may have said, thought, or done wrong. Guilt can also show up if you had intentions and did not take action. The Guilty self is partners with the Procrastinator self, which encourages self-sabotage.

As with every Fallen Angel, there is a gift inside, and the gift your Guilty self offers is to remember your Loving Self. Your Guilty self will red flag you if your actions are not in alignment with your deepest core values. When you experience guilt, you are criticizing yourself and making yourself wrong instead of learning from the experience. With every action you take you are given an opportunity to learn more about yourself. If you do not like the actions you have taken in the past, now you have an opportunity to course correct next time.

Guilt can also stop a person from taking necessary and constructive action in the present moment such as a parent who feels guilty for divorcing her or his spouse. This guilt may cause her or him to be more of a friend to the children than follow through with the discipline and guidance they actually need.

Life is about learning, unlearning and relearning. With every action you discover what works and what does not. With every behavior you discover what repels people and what behaviors create connection. With every experience you awaken to who you are not and who you really are.

You have the power to rewrite your past by seeing the gift in all experience. When you listen to your inner higher guidance, you will do things for others because you *want to* and not because you feel you *have to*. Forgive yourself for who you *were* and focus on who you are *now*. When your behavior and actions are in alignment with your values, you will have released the vibration of guilt. This is a journey and requires much patience. Regret also disappears when you view every moment as a learning opportunity

As long as you carry the *seed* of guilt, your Guilty self will keep you locked up in the past. It is time to tell your Guilty self you are setting yourself free from resentment, shame, regret and guilt because you know everything has happened for your highest good. You are now making the choice to take inspired action and align with the higher energies of self-acceptance, self-honor, and self-love.

Remember, your past is not always about you. You are also a Divine messenger and everything you did in your past was helping others learn about themselves. If you were mean, cruel or rude you were there to remind others of where they are vibrating in life. You were also mirroring aspects of themselves they did not love. You were assisting others to evolve, to say no to fear, or to wake up to their spirituality or deepen into personal growth or to detach from those who do not respect them. You may have been assisting others in opening their hearts to compassion and understanding. You have no idea how your words, actions and behaviors were a necessary part of another's evolution, or the catalyst necessary for them to spiral up and raise their vibration into higher worlds of love, support and connection.

Today's Higher Idea: What if you could let go of the idea that you made any mistakes in the past? What if you discovered that your *God Self* or *Goddess Self* wanted to experience everything through you, just for the sake of experiencing life on earth from one spectrum to the other?

Higher Idea #22 Forgive Your Angry Self

Do you react or respond to life? We are idea-creating, opinion-forming, and decision-making beings. How you deal with everyday problems and stresses is always up to you. We all have an Angry self and if we do not acknowledge this inner Fallen Angel it can destroy harmony in relationships both personally and professionally. The Angry self is an accumulation of all incorrect thoughts that are locked in a vibration with the physical body and also within the collective consciousness. This self takes everything personally and thrives on disrupting peace, connection with others, and rebels against higher learning.

The Angry self enjoys being right and making everyone wrong. This self also *thrives* on being in control and having power over others by forcing others to listen to its ranting and raving and making sure it is understood…or else! This Fallen Angel is deeply afraid of having a heart to heart conversation, and it will sabotage any sign of intimacy as intimacy involves vulnerability and losing control.

The Angry self reacts in frustration and cannot handle the smallest amount of stress. The Angry self has expectations of how people *should* respond or act in a certain way and when they don't, this *self* reacts. It doesn't take much for something to raise our blood pressure when people don't behave how we think they should. It can be anything from someone cutting us off on the freeway to a simple misunderstanding. We then justify our thoughts in an attempt to explain our reactions. We find reasons for being angry and frustrated, and as long as we are hanging on to the victim story of our past or blaming others for how our life is, we will feel powerless.

This Fallen Angel believes that others are to blame for what has happened to you instead of allowing you to be accountable for your own feelings and experiences. This Fallen Angel is very insecure and constantly creates misunderstandings. I am sure you have noticed yourself and other people go through an irrational set of actions because of an issue that surfaced. It means a memory has been re-stimulated, causing a person to react instead of respond to a situation.

If your Angry self is constantly lashing out and sabotaging the goodness in your life, it means you have allowed one cherry out of your entire Divine cherry pie to take over. This voice within your mind will always tell you lies, and if you let it, it will turn the smallest issue into the biggest war zone. It is time to take your power back.

You may be unaware of your behavior in the moment when a Fallen Angel takes over your mind. However, that is when you have the most need to pay attention to it. Every issue helps you expand your awareness of these inner selves that control you like a puppet. Remember, as long as the Angry self is in control of your life, tragedies or unpleasant situations may arise, forcing you to open your heart. It is time to gain your power back so you can see the gift in all things, for within every crisis is a gift, a reason for the experience.

This Fallen Angel has not been taught how to respond to life from an emotionally mature place as it reflects the child within who feels unloved and unappreciated. Yes, your Angry self may direct blame at others in your life; however, the truth is, your Angry self is angry with you for not living fully and ignoring your own passion and dreams.

You are on this planet to direct the many *selves* within and begin the journey of integration. When you learn how to listen to what your Fallen Angels need or want from you (*which is self-love*), you'll discover there is light at the end of every tunnel.

To transform an Angry self into a *Remembered Angel* requires awareness, inner reflection, acknowledgment, and a willingness to transform one's behavior. I will share more in upcoming chapters on how to deepen into greater *self*-love for all the Fallen Angels alive inside of you.

All perceived negative emotions represent a lack of self-love, self-worth, self forgiveness and self-respect. You are being called right now to become personally responsible for how you feel without guilt, shame or blame. When this happens your world will transform completely.

Today's Higher Idea: When you feel anger, you are only ever angry with yourself. Always apologize for venting and spewing toxic energy on the ones you love, and follow through with a random act of kindness. The *Divine Mind Conversation* (Higher Idea #79) is a powerful way to release your anger.

Higher Idea #23 Say Goodbye to Your Addictive Self

Since I am not a doctor or psychologist, I can only share my own experience of how I allowed my Addictive self to control my life. In this book's introduction, I mentioned I suffered with drug and alcohol addictions in my early twenties. I felt so alone then, and the only way I felt connected or had a sense of belonging was in the company of people who liked to party non-stop. It was only in this world of toxicity that I felt invincible. I believe most substance abusers have a similar motivation.

Many organizations and options are available to aid in transforming these addictions; however, I did it without the help of any group or organization. I simply went within and began the process of aligning with my Divine Mind and communicating with my Addictive self who had really taken over the Divine cherry pie of my life. My Addictive self felt empty, was very needy, and was always seeking unhealthy ways to fill up the void. This Fallen Angel created a belief within me that I needed cigarettes, alcohol, and drugs to feel *something* other than the emotional pain. I did not know how to feel happy naturally.

The Addictive self believes that the only way to move through a life of hell, chaos, struggle, pain, or loneliness or to feel a sense of control is with a man-made product such as coffee, cigarettes, refined sugar, processed food, drugs, or alcohol. One of these will make the emotional and mental pain go away. It does, but only temporarily.

If the Addictive self remains in control, it can destroy intimacy in relationships because it can drive you away from your beloved and into a fantasy world of pornography and sexual affairs.

Give yourself a gift and let go of the idea that you need to grasp obsessively at something external to feel *full!* The fullness you seek is spiritual fulfillment. When you face your Addictive self and discover the truth that all this *self* craves is your LOVE, self-love, you'll realize that your cravings have nothing to do with what is outside of your body. Self-love (*selves love*) is all any of your Fallen Angels crave. It is your acknowledgment that they exist that will turn your life around. Your soul wants you to remember that it's there, *inside of you.* Turn your focus to the knowledge that your Divine nature is calling and that you have an extraordinary inner power that can transform your life and turn all the mental and emotional pain into the peace and happiness you seek. You have legions of angels waiting to assist you through your darkest times.

We are here to enjoy and experience everything! We are here to eat and enjoy chocolate, great sex, money, and all the things that give us pleasure. At the same time, we need to stay centered in our power as Divine human beings. We are to obtain self-mastery within the physical world—not to be controlled by it.

Today's Higher Idea: Ask yourself, "Do I control what goes into my body? Am I allowing human-made products such as tobacco, alcohol, or food to control me? If I am on the path to loving myself, is what I am doing to my body a reflection of that love?"

Higher Idea #24 Remember Your Inner Forgotten Angels

I have defined what your Fallen Angels are, so now, let's take a look at your inner Forgotten Angels. Your Forgotten Angels represent your positive emotions or higher states of mind, such as love, joy, bliss, happiness, purpose, health, and all the higher vibrations of energy that live above the line in the *Freedom Frequency* Chart (Higher Idea #4).

Our Forgotten Angels carry Divine intelligence, and I refer to them as the Forgotten Angels because these are aspects of ourselves that we have forgotten. As human beings, we have forgotten our Divine nature. We have forgotten that happiness, passion, bliss, abundance, health, and love are our natural state of being. Every desirable state or quality lives inside of us, and it is up to us to remember.

To connect with your Forgotten Angels, I suggest you visualize them as higher versions of who you are, such as: your Brilliant Self, your Loving Self, your Joyful Self, your Godman Self, your Goddess Self, your Wise Self, your Passionate Self, Your Healthy Self, and so on. You get the higher idea here, right?

Now you may have noticed that I use an uppercase 'Self' when referring to a Forgotten Angel such as your Brilliant Self and I use a lowercase 'self' when referring to your Fallen Angels such as your Angry self. Upper and lower says it all.

Okay, moving on. It's time to dive in and discover the secrets of your spiritual dimension. When expanding your perceptions about who you are and what your true reality is, you may experience resistance. All resistance, fear, darkness, and ego is associated with your Fallen Angels who live below the line. Acceptance, love, light, and soul are associated with your Forgotten Angels who live above the line.

For example, your Forgotten Angels carry the seeds of appreciation, joy, love, and respect required to create the fulfilling relationship you seek. For instance, once you connect to your Joyful Self, you will want to bring more joy into your beloved's experience. When you connect to your Happy Self, you will naturally have a desire to bring happiness into your relationship. You will remember the joyful and happy person your beloved once was and the joyful and happy person you once were. This is the path to restoring the love that you once had. As you focus more on the good and why you embraced love with each other in the first place, you will attract and experience more of the good that has always been there.

Your Forgotten Angels will also assist you in your business. I have imagined my Forgotten Angels like the Knights of the Round Table, here to serve for the highest good of all human kind. I have visualized them to be my *inner* Board of Directors who suggests insights and higher perspectives. Through this creative visualization process, I have received profound information that has guided me and my business to where I am today.

When you acknowledge and integrate these Forgotten Angels who carry higher thought forms of information, they will assist you in transforming your Fallen Angels and help you take back your power as a Divine human being.

Today's Higher Idea: Write a list of what makes your *beloved* happy. If you don't know, *ask*. Write a list of what makes you happy. Now share your lists and take steps that create laughter, joy, and peace even when you don't want to. Heart-centered actions create a smile and have the power to take you to a new level of being together.

Higher Idea #25 Embrace Your Tears

When you say, "Yes" to Emotional Integrity you are saying, "Yes" to being fully present and accountable for how you feel.

Have you been afraid to feel the energy that is ALIVE inside of you? When was the last time you allowed yourself to *cry* fully? I mean really allowed yourself the time and space to *sob* until you experienced a place of inner peace?

With all life losses, there is a grieving process. Unfortunately, many of us have been taught to avoid the grieving process so all these hurtful feelings are deposited into the subconscious mind with the hope that they will be forgotten. If we continue to ignore our feelings, the suppression of these heavy energies within the body will eventually explode in anger or rage, causing external destruction in our relationships and/or put the body in a state of *dis-ease*. Emotions do not have to overwhelm us if we make the healthy choice to honor how we feel in every moment.

When the pain of life is so intense, you may want to shut down completely. I am asking you to resist the urge to do so. This does not mean you have to relive each hurtful experience. In order for any emotional pain to be transformed, you need to shift through your resistance and allow the full expression of your emotional pain to be acknowledged in a healthy way. I am here to assist you in learning how to let go through the transformative power of *tears*.

Tears are the most powerful cleansing mechanism your physical body has. Accepting your feelings is a huge step in taking your power back. Tears offer the space to shift your beliefs and recreate new empowering choices. Ultimately, tears strengthen your inner core as they cleanse your memory banks of all stored experiences that hold a negative energetic charge to your past.

Everything that is not built on truth will eventually collapse. Tears are the crumbling of an illusion, the grieving of a perceived loss. On the other side of tears is where you recognize the truth of who you are, your own Divine nature.

Your emotions carry important information, and if you do not listen to the energies that move through you, you may take a path that will not serve your highest good. Allowing your emotions to be experienced as energy moving through you without judging the sensation as wrong or right, good or bad, brings forth your wisdom and opens up the prison gates. Trapped energy in your body can be released through the natural and transformative process of *tears*.

Have you ever cried and afterwards, felt depressed and lost? Now you can learn how to free your tears and, at the same time, feel empowered on the other side of those tears. Underneath your anger, sadness and fear is your Divinity. The only reason you are angry, sad or fearful is because you have forgotten the light, the connection to Source that lives inside of you.

To be an empowered human being, you are asked to tune in with your vibrational energetic emotional landscape. This means to expand your awareness of how you feel 100 percent of the time. When you shed tears it means you are ready to disarm, to drop the sword, to end the fight, and drop the armor around your heart. Give yourself a powerful gift of an emotional release through the shedding of tears. Your inner strength is on the other side of your emotional vulnerability.

Emotional Integrity brings emotional maturity which brings the realization that deep down our sadness is a reflection of how much we have lost touch with our connection to the Universe. We have turned our focus onto people and created judgments about their flaws or faults instead of focusing on what truly matters. Your tears are designed to help you remember.

If you want to experience more love in your life, or deeper and more meaningful relationships, whether personally or in business, then it is time for you to become accountable for how you *feel* and seek a healthier expression in releasing your emotions.

Today's Higher Idea: Check out the Emotional Integrity Process in the Resource section.

Chapter Three
Peace of Mind

As much as transforming your emotions is key to living a happier life, it is also important to know that your mind plays a big role in your quest for happiness and freedom. These higher states of mind can only ever be experienced when your mind is at peace with itself.

Peace of mind is a gift you give yourself. To have your thoughts transform from a chaotic state to calmness is a discipline anyone can learn. It is in the stillness of your mind that all duality—positive and negative, good and bad, right and wrong—dissolve.

The reason for all external conflict is simply a reflection of the internal conflict between the many internal selves, your Fallen Angels and your Soul.

Your Fallen Angels, the invisible dimensions of you, seek your acknowledgment, love, and understanding. As long as they remain fragmented or unwanted, their voices, those negative thoughts and beliefs, will continually sabotage your happiness and dreams. They will not give you the peace of mind you seek. Only when you acknowledge their existence, learn to forgive, love, and integrate their energy into the light of awareness will your mind begin to calm. If you crave peace in your life, start today by connecting your Fallen Angels (mind) with your Forgotten Angels (heart).

Higher Idea #26 Dive Into Your Mind

Many years ago, I had a friend and mentor named Steven. He was a very wise man and shared with me the importance of knowing one's mind. When explaining the mind, he often referred to Sigmund Freud's theory of personality, using the iceberg analogy; however, my friend embraced a more spiritual approach, which I completely resonated with. He would ask me to use my imagination and see my mind as if it were an iceberg floating in an ocean. Now I ask you to do the same.

The part of the iceberg that is visible, above the waterline, is the smallest part of the iceberg. Your conscious mind represents the smallest part of the iceberg. Your conscious mind represents the level of awareness you have of your present reality. Your conscious mind can only think one thought at a time.

Below the water line, the iceberg is vast, and the same is true of your subconscious mind. Your subconscious mind is mostly unknown until you dive deep and explore its depths.

Your subconscious mind has many layers and is capable of storing every thought, wish, desire, habit, attitude, feeling, and memory from this life—past, parallel, and beyond. Your subconscious mind also controls the natural functions of your body such as circulation, respiration, and digestion. Just as your body functions are on automatic pilot, so too are your behavior patterns.

The third aspect of your mind, I call your *Divine Mind*, which is like an ocean of flowing intelligence. Your Divine Mind is the gateway to Universal Consciousness or the Source of All That Is, which is experienced in deep trance or meditation. This is where you connect to the genius or Brilliant Self that lives within you.

Your experience in the physical world is played out through these three phases, and within each phase are many layers of complexity. To understand your mind fully, it may take many lifetimes. For now, you are on an evolutionary journey from living with a fear-based mind to spiraling up and embodying your Divine Mind which plays a big role in living a heart-centered life.

Today's Higher Idea: Talk to a friend about what you are learning.

Higher Idea #27 Put Your Ego in its Place

Your *ego* handles life's issues in three ways; fight, flee, or freeze. Any time you choose any of these three ways of reacting, you are living in the Fear Frequency. Your subconscious mind will brand every experience as a negative experience if your Fallen Angels (your ego) is in control. Your ego is not a monster. It is more like a frightened child and has been given way too much responsibility.

As I mentioned earlier, your subconscious mind is where all your unacceptable, hidden, or fragmented *selves* exist (your inner Fallen Angels). The "ego" and your many Fallen Angels are synonymous. Unfortunately, if you operate your whole life from the ego perspective, you will experience pain and suffering because the ego's purpose is to keep you living in your small comfort zone as it believes you need to be protected from everything outside of your comfort zone. Your ego believes life is dangerous, so it will do whatever it takes to keep you separated from the truth. Now you may want to destroy or get rid of your ego; however, I would suggest a higher idea, which is to put it back in its place of *processing information only* and to stop it from controlling your life.

Every time you say to yourself, "I am fat," "I am stupid," or "I am a loser," you are feeding your ego. Your subconscious mind takes everything you say as truth and goes about creating the reality around you to support your beliefs. This is why it is so important to dismantle any and all negative beliefs you have about yourself and your life. You are a Divine Human Being of the Universe and there is no one like you.

Transformation begins with self-awareness about who you are. You have the power to change your mind at any time about anything with ease and grace. You do have control of the thoughts you think, and when you discover this truth, you raise your vibration.

To take control of your fear-based mind, your *ego*, you are required to reprogram it just as you would a computer. Reprogramming requires influencing your subconscious mind at a cellular or vibrational level, so that new empowering truths can be imprinted.

To reprogram a negative state of mind into a higher state of mind is to embrace your spirituality, the higher aspects of who you are. Remember that you are a brilliant human being, that you are the creator of your life, and that you can be, do, and have whatever you wish. Your subconscious mind was designed to be of service to you, not the other way around.

In order to *happy* about yourself and your life, it is essential that you create happiness within your mind first. Happiness is realized when you give your life meaning.

A powerful way to direct your *ego* is to invite the higher energies of your Divine Mind into your heart, which will activate your heart's intelligence. Then visualize the higher frequencies of light and color entering into every cell of your body to reactivate your soul's blueprint. The *Divine Mind Conversation* will remind you to speak to your subconscious mind with assertiveness, clarity, absolute love and respect. Your subconscious mind is here to serve you and as you make the unknown aspect of yourself *known,* you empower yourself.

Another powerful way of directing your mind to a higher vibration and create more happiness in your life is to release all words from your vocabulary that carry a negative vibration and replace them with higher vibrational words or statements. (I discuss this more in Chapter 5.)

If you think back to a disagreement you had with someone can you see where your frustration or anger compounds turning the smallest issue into a mountain of blame? It is because the *ego* will show you images of all the similar scenarios of the past, on all the wrong things this person has done, instead of just focusing on today's issue. Your *ego* loses control the more you stay in the present moment, surrender to *what is* and focus on what you need to learn about yourself. In fact, letting go of the idea that you *need to be right* will put your ego in its place which is…processing information only…Now you have the power to shift your mind to a higher state of awareness.

Today's Higher Idea: Talk about what you are learning about yourself and how you have allowed your *ego* to control your life.

Higher Idea #28 Create an Empowered Life Story

Have you defined which Fallen Angels live inside of you and the story they bring into your life? As I mentioned in Chapter Two, your Fallen Angels are fragmented *selves* that represent a collective of suppressed intelligent energy. These unwanted *selves* do not want to be trapped in your physical body, and they may be the reason why you act and behave inappropriately at times. All of these inner selves represent soul fragments and each one carries a story. A story of "I am not good enough", or "I am not worthy", or "I was abused and now I am unlovable", or "I always fail so what is the use", and so on.

Our mind can become divided or fragmented when we have experienced emotional trauma or suffering. We can portray our external self as being strong, powerful, and self-confident in a business meeting or in front of our family and friends when actually, deep inside, there is that little girl or boy who is feeling alone, afraid, and unloved.

Exploring the many *selves* (fallen and forgotten) and acknowledging their existence will offer you the profound gifts of inner wisdom and insight (*inner sight*) you may have been seeking. Now you have an opportunity to acknowledge the "poor me" story you may have been living out and recreate a new empowered story.

Peace of mind comes when you have released the chaotic, incorrect thinking that is attached to your old stories. Stories of blame, shame, and guilt will keep you vibrating in the lower realm of fear-based living. Stories of how life is so unfair, hard, difficult, ugly, and miserable will keep you in the muck and chained to a reality created by limiting or false beliefs.

Right now, in this very moment you have the power to focus on a new empowered story. A story where all you see is the power you have in creating a beautiful life because you now have a beautiful mind. A story where all you see is beautiful souls who have fallen into a pit of darkness only to awaken to the truth of who they are.

Your imagination is the key to creating a new personal and global story that empowers humanity. As you develop your courage and take the journey beyond the familiar and explore the deepest parts of your mind, body and soul, you begin to expand your sphere of what is possible for you and for all of us.

Your Fallen Angels also live in your physical body and create the stories of physical pain and suffering. If your body is filled with fear it will not be able to heal itself. When you release a Fallen Angel you not only liberate your mind you also liberate your body and the limited story that your 'dis-ease' is who you are.

When you're in unknown territory, such as exploring your mind, it's always a good idea to have a guide with you, someone you can trust. Your Brilliant Self is always up for a great adventure and is the best of all possible companions. It is your Divine Mind that will introduce you to your Joyful Self, your Creative Self, your Prosperity Self, and your Purposeful Self. As you intentionally connect, embrace and eventually integrate with these higher levels of consciousness your life begins to take on a whole new meaning.

So how do you know when you have let go of your wounded stories of the past? When you no longer talk about past events or people in a negative way. When you focus on what is happening right here, right now. When you choose to talk about the vision you have in creating a harmonious world. This will definitely raise your vibration and level of consciousness.

You can make a quantum leap and spiral up into the *Freedom Frequency* when you make the choice to acknowledge, listen, appreciate, and love all your Fallen and Forgotten Angels that live inside of you. Your Fallen Angels will tell you all the false stories you have held on as truth and your Forgotten Angels will remind you of the empowered story that lives in your heart. They have a great deal to teach you.

Today's Higher Idea: Identify your "poor me" stories of unworthiness, lack and self rejection. You are being called to close the old book of your life and open a new book and write out your new empowered story.

Higher Idea #29 Dismantle Your Limited Beliefs

Have you ever had to pack up all your belongings and move to another city or even across the country? Even if you were moving just across town, you would most likely have many boxes filled with your most valuable possessions. Sometimes people move several times during their lives. It's a lot of work, involving time as well as organizational skills needed for all the unpacking and clearing out of all the boxes.

How would you feel if you never unpacked or removed those boxes? What if you just lived with those boxes cluttering your space the rest of your life, not knowing what was in them?

This is what you do with your beliefs. Throughout your life, you have created beliefs (decisions you made about who you are and the reality you live in), and then you placed these beliefs in boxes in your mind and then forgot about them. Beliefs can become like cluttered cardboard boxes, filling the mansion of your mind.

Your belief system is programmed from:

- What you have been told to believe from your parents, teachers, friends, and/or the media.
- Observations you deem as truth.
- What you tell yourself every moment.

The reality you experience is kept in place by a belief structure. Beliefs are not necessarily true. For example, people once believed the world was flat until someone expanded their world. People once believed it was impossible that televisions or computers would be in every home. Your belief system can create illusions or truth, lack or abundance, or they can create resistance or expand love. Your belief system is either working *against* you or *for* you.

In order for your belief system to work *for* you and create the life you want, I highly recommend you become aware of the limited beliefs still stored in your belief mansion. With every piece you don't let go of, you hold yourself back from becoming the person you want to be. The mind becomes filled with outdated ideas and dysfunctional decisions that leave no room for a new expanded sense of Self. Change in your outer life begins when you transform your inner self (selves) and integrate them with Source energy, with your Divine Mind.

Expanding your awareness of what you believe, how you think, what you say, and how you act is key to changing limiting behavior patterns. It's time to believe and connect with your Forgotten Angels as they carry the highest vibrations and hold the key to the truth of who you are.

Confidence grows the more you *believe* in yourself, in your Higher Selves who live above the line. Keep your focus on what you're good at and nurture these higher qualities. Remember, you are not your parents. You are here to become the person you want to be. Go within and you will find your answers.

Once you set your mind on where you want to go, life will give you many opportunities to practice, practice, practice. My dad would always say to me, "I believe in you Karen, but more importantly, I want you to believe in yourself; no matter what challenges life brings, never give up!"

Years ago, I was watching a *Loving Relationship* video by Dr. Gary Smalley. As I was watching him and the impact he had on his audience, I knew I wanted to become a speaker. Yet at that time, I was deathly afraid of speaking in public as I had a limited belief I would never be good enough or smart enough. The first time I went to a Toastmasters group and had to introduce myself, I could barely get the words out. It took a lot of time and inner work in clearing out my negative beliefs but it was worth it. Today, I speak in front of large audiences and instead of fear holding me back, I feel a thrill in being of service and sharing my passion. My point is, even though you may not be aware of your purpose, your greatest talent may be hiding behind your greatest fear.

Today's Higher Idea: What do you believe in? What beliefs do you have about yourself and your ability to raise your vibration and live a heart-centered life?

Higher Idea #30 Face Your Fear

Do you know you have secret fears that can hold you back from living your life fully? We all do, until we embrace the courage to consciously explore our own mind from a higher point of view. Acknowledging your fear is the first step in releasing the chains that may bind you. Before a list of fears can be presented, let's first define *fear*. Fear is defined as *the anticipation of pain*. Fear is also an acronym, *False Evidence Appearing Real*.

At the core of the Fear Frequency is your *ego* and your *ego* is in control of all your Fallen Angels. Your *ego* does not want you to discover these aspects of yourself. Why? Because it will lose control and you will become empowered. Your *ego* wants you to stay in the vibration of self-denial, self-rejection, self-doubt and self-hatred. It does not want you to look at your *self*, or the many *selves* within because then you will discover who you are beyond the *self*.

Fear has become a powerful energy force on our planet because of the accumulation of fear-based thinking within the collective consciousness that has had thousands of years to gain power. Fear in itself is—*an illusion of your mind*. When you are in fear, you allow your imagination to work "against" you instead of "for" you. The key is remembering that you are not your fear. Instead, begin to see it as energy that moves through you. Fear in itself is not a bad thing because it allows you to be cautious and proceed slowly so you can understand your experiences. However, when you choose to live in the present moment and express love, then you no longer need the energy of fear to be your teacher. This is not about you becoming fearless; this is about you becoming deliciously free.

There are a range of secret fears we have suppressed within our subconscious mind, such as the fear of rejection, fear of loneliness, fear of embarrassment, fear of lack, fear of judgment, fear of losing control, fear of being left behind, fear of being found out, fear of betrayal, fear of pain, fear of loss, fear of what others think, fear of letting go, fear of abandonment, fear of intimacy, fear of not being loved, fear of being wrong, fear of being persecuted for your beliefs, fear of conflict, and fear of your Light. There are many more fears to add to the list, however; this is a good place to start.

Today's Higher Idea: Identify the fear you're ready to face and release.

Higher Idea #31 Self-Discipline is About Learning

Many of us cringe upon hearing the word *discipline*; it just sounds so rigid and definitely not fun. Did you know that *"discipline"* and *"disciple"* are based on the same root word which means *to learn?* Self-discipline is inner motivation and not about controlling others or a means of punishment. Self-discipline is the *focused attention* needed to change your life for the better. You can read about great ideas and strategies that may benefit you, but it takes effort, trust, and courage to act and integrate these principles on a daily basis.

Self-discipline can be seen as a process of devotion in improving all areas of your life and honoring the totality of who you are mentally, spiritually, emotionally, and physically. If your thoughts are scattered, if you are easily triggered to anger, or procrastinate on projects, then discipline of thought, behavior and action will be required to follow through with decisions that can better your life. Choose to see self-discipline as the path that leads you to greater pleasures in life. A great quote I love (author unknown) is, "Discipline is making the choice between what you want now and what you want the most." For example, self-discipline is when a person who wants a relationship to last will stop the destructive behaviors that are destroying it.

When you take control of your mental dimension and put your mind in order, you will experience less chaos. Everything in the Universe works together. By educating yourself, you'll learn that the primary law of creation is *order*. Even though life may appear to be chaotic at the core, there is order—*a reason for everything we experience.* Even traffic jams appear to be chaotic, but every driver has a destination.

Today's Higher Idea: View self-discipline as self-love or self-devotion to a higher way of living.

Higher Idea #32 Breathe in the Energy of Patience

Have you ever had a mental meltdown? Have you been confused as to why things are not happening the way you want them to? Have you stomped around yelling at the Universe, *What's going on now? I shouldn't have to do this. This shouldn't be happening to me. I am a good person. I want my beautiful life NOW!* I have said these exact words many times. I believe we all have moments of ranting and raving when a dream is not being realized or we just don't seem to be manifesting what we want.

Freedom is a choice, and becoming free requires patience. Patience is not about waiting. Patience is required to move from the world you live in now to the world you want to create. Patience is the gap between the current *you* and the Brilliant YOU *(the butterfly analogy I mention in the introduction)* that is waiting to emerge. Patience is the space required for deep reflection as you take the journey in remembering your Divine nature.

Children and seniors are fabulous teachers of patience. You will also know you have cultivated patience when you no longer experience road rage. Everyone is showing you the path to staying in the present moment which is where your power lies. Whether you are waiting for others or waiting for a dream to be realized, it is in those moments of waiting that you are being called to reflect on any incompletions or unresolved issues that need to be addressed or acted upon.

The practice of daily meditation and deep breathing will also empower you in fully embracing the energy of patience. In patience, we allow the many invisible selves to blossom and transform. When you are patient with yourself, you will then experience patience with others.

I also recommend you practice the *Divine Mind Conversation* (Higher Idea #79) to help you remember your Patient Self.

Today's Higher Idea: Whenever you feel you do not have the willingness or tolerance for delay, see this as an opportunity for deep reflection on present issues in your life. Smile! Tell yourself that you are choosing to be a patient person as this is how you want others to be with you.

Higher Idea #33 Breathe in the Energy of Trust

In order for you to experience integration with any of your Forgotten Angels that live above the line, you will first need to breathe in the energy of trust. The energy of trust carries a firm belief in who you are as a Divine human being. Trust in yourself. Trust in others. Trust in the universe.

Trust transforms belief into knowing and then knowing into remembering. Trust is having the knowledge that you possess the inner strength and ability to move through every situation or opportunity that life offers you. Trust is having the knowledge that whatever you attract in your life is guiding you to a higher learning. The world of trust is very powerful, and your Trusting Self will take you on a most incredible journey to deeper worlds beyond the physical dimension.

As you remember the power of trust and breathe it into your heart center, you will trust yourself and the world around you. In order to experience trust in others, trust must blossom within you. As you deepen into you're your spiritual journey and breathe in trust, you will remember that the universe is safe and supportive.

The more you align and create a relationship with your Forgotten Angels, the more you'll trust the inner voice of wisdom, the voice of Intuition. Trust that no matter what happens, you are meant to experience it for the evolution of Self. A person who trusts herself/himself can quickly make a decision, get off the fence, and move forward knowing that whichever direction she or he has chosen will be a great adventure.

Today's Higher Idea: Trust that you are always safe and the universe supports and loves you.

Higher Idea #34 Remember Your Divine Mind

Your Divine Mind is the cosmic upper realm that envelops both the conscious and subconscious minds. Your Divine Mind is where your inner Forgotten Angels resonate and your connection to All That Is.

Remember, your subconscious mind does not transform with your conscious mind. Your subconscious transforms more rapidly when your Divine Mind is utilized and linked to your emotional dimension. In other words, when you connect your imagination with the power of higher thought vibrations and emotions, you can then explore your subconscious as an empowered human being and transform all limitation into freedom.

Your Divine Mind exists in the realm of pure genius; it's all around and within you. It's quite literally *everywhere* and the core essence of your Divine Mind is enlightened love and harmony. This realm carries the information of your soul's purpose, and the blueprint of your Brilliant Self, the highest version of you. This is where all insights, ideas and creative sparks of genius exist, all waiting for you to consciously align your vibration to this realm of Divinity and access to Source energy.

You are either operating from your fear-based mind which keeps you in your limitation or you are operating from your Divine Mind which is the journey beyond the familiar. Your Divine Mind will always take you outside of your comfort zone and beyond the radar screen of your mind as this is where all manifested dreams reside.

Harmony of mind consists of exploring the unknown subconscious mind and Divine mind and bringing them into your conscious awareness. Here you develop intimacy (into-me-I-see) with your inner Fallen Angels and your Forgotten Angels which transforms them both into Remembered Angels, the light of who you are.

Today's Higher Idea: State out loud, *"With divine intention I now ask my Brilliant Self to show me the way and help me to release all fear and negative energies from my mind consciousness system now with ease and grace. I ask my Brilliant Self to download the information I require in moving forward in the direction of my heart desires. And so it is."* Now let go and trust that you will receive the guidance you are seeking.

Chapter Four
Open Your Brilliant Heart

Have you lived your life with a guarded heart or an open heart? Many of us have closed our hearts from fear of being hurt again. The walls will keep out the hurt and pain, but they also keep out the love and joy we are seeking.

A heart that is guarded or closed heart is unable to fulfill the dream it is here to realize and will also hold you back from connecting to all your Forgotten Angels that live in the higher vibratory realms such as your Joyful Self, your Loving Self, your Sensual Self, your Passionate Self, and so on. The loneliness and unnecessary suffering you experience is caused from the separation from Source, an absence of love, the absence of love you have for yourself (*selves*).

The walls around your heart are created by your Fallen Angels, the voices within that say, "Do not trust men/women" or "Love means getting hurt" or "Love is painful." If you believe this, you have been deceived into believing a lie. It is the lower thought forms that reside in the Fear Frequency that breed manipulation, betrayal, and neglect. When you are in the Freedom Frequency of life, you will only attract respectful and honest people who deeply care and wish only the best for you.

Your heart is very intelligent. New research from The Institute of

HeartMath (see Resources section) states that the heart is the most powerful generator of electromagnetic energy in the human body, producing the largest rhythmic electromagnetic field of any of the body's organs. The heart's electrical field is about sixty times greater in amplitude than the electrical activity generated by the brain. The magnetic field produced by the heart is more than 5,000 times greater in strength than the field generated by the brain, and it can be detected a number of feet away from the body.

You are being called to expand your capacity to receive more love. If you have ever experienced heartache it is because your heart is actually expanding, breaking open to *self* and deepening into s*elf-love.*

When you become consciously aware of the power you possess in your heart, all your challenges, issues, and shortcomings will dissolve to the size of an atom. Your heart has the intelligence to bring forth all you desire with ease and grace. When your heart and mind are aligned, you are divinely powerful. With the practice of meditation, breath work, visualization, and devotion, you have the power to release all perceived negative forces from your heart center so that you can live a heart-centered life. When your heart is fully open to the nurturing qualities of giving and receiving *love,* you are *free.* The effort is worth it.

Living a heart-centered life begins by embracing self-love, then relationship love, then community love, and then we expand to global love and unite in universal love.

Higher Idea #35 Live in Enlightened Love

As I mentioned in Chapter One, the core essence of the *Freedom Frequency* is *love*. This love does not compare to physical love, romantic love, sexual love, or friendship love. It is a higher love I refer to as *enlightened love*. Enlightened love is like having heaven awaken inside of you and all pain, negative thoughts, and feelings vanish completely, leaving you in a state that is beyond bliss and beyond any physical happiness you may have experienced. Enlightened love the glue that binds everything. It is an expanded awareness or state of being where you see the personality of others, and yet at the same time, you acknowledge the divinity (the soul) within every human being. You will know you are resonating in the vibration of enlightened love when you meet someone and all you see is another version of yourself standing before you. You have remembered that you are *one* with all of life.

You may have experienced a taste of this higher love on occasion when you have a direct spiritual experience in meditation or in sharing an extraordinary experience with others. To fully live in this higher vibration of love, one must take the journey in disciplining the ego, the Fallen Angels within. Compassionate discipline stirred with the devotion of spiritual fulfillment is a path anyone can take toward embracing the higher vibrations of enlightened love.

As much as you crave love, you may find yourself hiding from it. Deep down, there may be an intense *fear* of love. Why? Because the *ego* does not want you to remember your own Divine nature. It will create an energetic wall of resistance every time you step into the light of higher love. *Enlightened love* is a high intensity vibration, and many of us have not been taught how to harness it. The vibration can feel uncomfortable because you are not used to feeling this powerful force move through your body. If you have been hiding for a long period of time in the darkness of the fear frequency, you can become so afraid of the unknown, of who you are, of where you are going, of connecting with others or of being *seen*. When the truth is, the only thing you are moving to is *love*, to being the *love*, to remembering you are LOVE.

Living in Enlightened Love is living in alignment with Source Energy and recognizing that all relationships are designed to empower. That is the main function of any relationship, which includes the relationships you have with your parents, children, siblings, friends, coworkers, partner, or spouse. All relationships are designed to empower you in becoming the best version of yourself.

How can you say you are in love with someone if you have yet to explore your own heart? To connect to the vibration of enlightened love you are called to listen to your heart, to release the bonds of yesterday and renew your own heart's intelligence.

The purpose of any relationship is to serve each other's growth and spiritual awakening. You attract people into your life for your own expansion, spiritually, mentally, emotionally, and physically. When each person in any relationship seeks to uplift the spirit instead of squashing the spirit, there is profound growth that occurs. Enlightened love relationships are experienced as a deep soul love for another and for life.

Many people are afraid of losing their identity in intimate relationships. The amazing thing is, you are meant to lose your identity, the identity of your *ego* so that you realign with your true identity as a Divine Human Being who is a powerful and heart-centered creator.

Every relationship you have with others reflects the relationship you have with yourself. If your relationship squashes your spirit in the form of constant arguing, blame, and criticism, it is time to take your power back. If you are squashing the spirit of others, then it is time to restore self-love. If you have the willingness to learn new and healthier ways of relating, you can re-ignite the spirit of empowerment in any relationship. The more you spiral up out of the fear frequency, the more your physical body becomes less dense, allowing the higher selves, your Forgotten Angels, to fill your body with the energies of *enlightened love*. You have the capacity to embody these eternal forces in your life by awakening your heart and remembering the brilliance that is you.

True freedom of being comes from diving deep into your subconscious mind, shifting perceptions of who you are, and spiraling up through your energy centers into your heart.

Today's Higher Idea: Your heart is wise; listen to it. When you make the choice to live from your heart, you will be empowered with a divine force of higher intelligence.

Higher Idea #36 Forgive Yourself

As I journeyed beyond the familiar and descended further down the stairs of my subconscious mind, I realized that my past would always haunt me until I had forgiven others and especially myself for all my perceived wrongdoings, lies and destructive behaviors. The path to forgiveness was not easy, but I knew in order for me to spiral up out of the fear frequency and into the Freedom Frequency, I needed to embody the energy of forgiveness. I struggled with forgiveness most of my life. I felt if I forgave the men who had raped me, I was making what they did to me okay. The hate I carried in my heart toward men consumed me. As much as I hated men, I wanted desperately to be in a relationship with a loving man. As my spirituality deepened, I realized that if I were to attract respectful and loving men into my life, I would first need to forgive the Masculine self within. I would also need to forgive and release the negative stories and beliefs I had wrapped around men.

Forgiving the men of my past included my ex-husband, cheating or abusive boyfriends, my father, my brother, and all *men* throughout time for their perceived wrongdoings of destruction, violence, abuse, neglect, and rape towards the feminine. This profound level of forgiveness was one of the biggest gifts I could ever give myself.

What I found more difficult was forgiving myself, which meant the acknowledgment of all *my* perceived wrongdoings, dark secrets, and the harm I may have caused others whether it was emotional, spiritual, or physical. The Emotional Integrity Process (see Resources section) allowed me to get real with the emotions and mental images I had suppressed in the many vaults of my memory banks. I sobbed uncontrollably as my life movie played before my mind's eye. I knew the hundreds of images that flashed before me were releasing all the negatively charged energy I had concealed. I even had surprising images surface as I saw my Inner Rapist, who showed me how I had raped women in a previous life. My Mean self, my Critical self and my Hateful self showed up as the mirrors of self-reflection. I heard the words, *"Everything I have done unto others, I will eventually experience myself."* I saw the karmic effects of all my actions and how every individual was playing his or her role so perfectly to reflect back how I saw myself. As the emotional pain subsided, I knew my Forgiving Self had found her way to me. I actually felt my energetic heart opening as I crossed the bridge of forgiveness and into enlightened love. My intention was to live in this state of bliss forever.

The energy of forgiveness opened me up and connected me to many of my Forgotten Angels who resided in the Freedom Frequency such as my Peaceful Self, my Respectful Self, my Compassionate Self, and my Loving Self. These *Selves*, who I had actually forgotten, showed me how to see my body differently, to love my body, and therefore, to respect and value myself wholly and completely.

The Unforgiving self lives below the line, refuses to forgive, and makes no allowance for error. The Unforgiving self carries the seed of all things *unforgiving,* and as long as this self remains in control, the heart will remain closed. To create a beautiful life, I suggest you connect to your Forgiving Self. Your Forgiving Self has the power to unlock the heavy chains that bind you to the fear frequency.

Forgiveness is the bridge from living in fear to crossing over and living in the Freedom Frequency of life. Self-forgiveness is key. Learning to forgive the many Fallen Angels that live inside of you and forgiving yourself for ignoring or rejecting these aspect of yourself, will open you up to the energy of *deservablity* to cross the bridge into the Freedom Frequency of life. Once you are above the line, there is nothing to forgive, as you are living in the love vibration.

Our past is just a memory, and memories are made up of moments. It is a moment in time that creates an experience, and then we judge that experience as either good/bad or right/wrong. If we deem the experience wrong, then our Protector self will show up and believe it needs to guard our heart. Our Protector self will then constantly remind us of this past moment in time by taking the same feeling about that one moment and making it our whole life story. When in reality, it was only a moment in time.

It is your Forgiving Self that will help you view your past from a higher perspective so you can recreate a new empowered memory of every moment. Every in your life who you believe has caused you grief, pain or suffering has come into your life to remind you to stop playing small, to stand up for yourself and live boldly in the direction of your dreams. Forgiveness blossoms when you know everyone is reflecting aspects of yourself you have yet to embrace.

Sometimes it's difficult to forgive, especially if you have lost your job, your home, or loved one. Once you embrace the world of forgiveness, you realize that it's a powerful means of cutting negative energy cords from others in your life. The more you forgive yourself and your own perceived negative behaviors and actions, the more you forgive the negative behaviors and actions (Fallen Angels) in others.

When you are living above the line, the energy of forgiveness is no longer necessary. There is nothing to forgive when you are vibrating in the *Freedom Frequency* of life, for here you are the embodiment of Compassion. It is here you recognize the divinity in yourself and divinity in others and everyone is fully accountable for every experience, thought, and feeling. You will only attract others who vibrate in the same frequency of thoughtfulness and compassion. Tragedy, drama, and trauma live below the line.

Today's Higher Idea: Become present to who you are *being*. Look in the mirror and make direct eye contact with yourself. Look deep into your eyes and say, *I love you. I'm sorry. Please forgive me. I appreciate you.*

Higher Idea #37 You Are a Valuable Human Being

See yourself as a valuable human being. Self-worth is increased when you connect to your *Worthy Self.* Your *Worthy Self* lives by a value system that is defined by you and not by the opinions of others. Your values are defined by what's important to you; for example, health, living authentically, freedom, service to others, creativity, love, and truth. Once you have established your core values—what is important to you—you can use them as a filter in making any important decision. Your values will help you filter people, business opportunities, or events. If you feel there is an alignment with your values, then proceed. If not, you know to move on.

Your values determine what kind of person you are. An important fact to remember is that your own sense of value is determined by what you believe about yourself and not by what you have. Remember, your goals and intentions need to be in alignment with your values; otherwise, you may need to change direction. A simple reality check to figure out where you're at in any given moment is to ask yourself, "Am I in alignment with my deepest core values?"

Only you can determine your own set of values and once you do, trust that they will always guide you in the right direction. When you integrate your values, you will make better and healthier choices based on your sense of self-worth. You will naturally lift your life up and attract people who resonate with the same values as you.

Remember, there is nothing more valuable in this world than YOU! You are a Divine Human Being of infinite power and potential.

Today's Higher Idea: Visit my website (see Resources section) to view a list of values. Write down five core values with which you feel you are in alignment. Use the *Divine Mind Conversation* method to connect to your Valuable Self and see what message is awaiting you.

Higher Idea #38 Nurture Your Soul

How often do you connect to your soul? Do you know it exists? How did you nurture your soul this week? There are many people who have no idea that their souls even exist. We all have a loving soul, born ready to embrace our earthly purpose, yet if our ego, our Fallen Angels, are allowed to rule, the soul is locked away, undernourished, and forgotten. The ego is determined to squash trust, imagination, and creativity, and it views vulnerability as a weakness. We may even build energetic walls around our heart in order to protect what we believe about ourselves.

Many people relate only to their own physical needs, wants, and desires, living with little or no regard for others. These individuals have yet to connect with their heart and soul. This is not wrong as every soul is awakening in divine time.

Right now consciousness is evolving and humanity is waking up and discovering a deeper sense of purpose; we have begun exploring the spiritual realms and deeper truths of our soul. By exploring the spiritual dimension, you discover the truth about who you are and the purpose of your existence. During this journey to the heart, many life lessons are learned and are essential if a higher love is to be realized.

Living above the line requires development of the soul. If your soul is under-developed, then your freedom of choice is limited. You always have the power to make necessary daily choices, but if you are making your decisions from a place of fear (ego), you may remain a victim of circumstance in which your only focus is personal survival and experiencing an unfulfilled life.

The day I woke up spiritually, I could not stop the tears from flowing. I had read books about the soul but now I was experiencing a profound part of me I never really knew existed before. I could not stop apologizing to my soul for ignoring it for so many years. My *soul* was like a long lost friend who knew everything about me and loved me unconditionally.

Today's Higher Idea: Place your attention on your heart and visualize a flame in the center. This flame symbolizes the *light of your soul*. It's up to you to ignite the light within and expand your soul power.

Higher Idea #39 Connect to Your Inner Child

Laughter, play, joy, fun, innocence and *being in the moment* are a few qualities your Inner Child can bring into your life. However, if you are not connected to this very real part of you, your life can be constantly influenced by an emotionally wounded Inner Child who inhabits an adult body. We all have an Inner Child, the aspect of us that holds the sum of all our childhood memories, and the more we tune into this aspect of ourselves we open the door to profound healing.

I believe there is a defining moment when a child experiences trauma and is not able to cope with the destructive energies in their environment, and therefore, in protecting itself the mind becomes fragmented, separating itself from reality. Our innocence, the Inner Child then hides deep down inside of us only to be possessed by the Protector self. This Fallen Angel may whisper, "Let me out and I will make you strong. You will never have to experience this sadness or loneliness again." Convinced that this inner voice is true, the frightened child says, "Yes," and the light of our innocence becomes buried. From this point forward, we grow up and live our life believing we are strong when in fact we're experiencing life through our Forgotten Inner Child who throws temper tantrums and bullies his/her way through life.

We unconsciously and unknowingly lock away our Inner Child as we take on the role of being an adult and all the responsibilities, stress, and expectations that go along with it. We become robots on automatic pilot. Meanwhile, our soul waits patiently for us to wake up to the innocent child within and remember the joy that lives in our heart.

This experience is a natural part of your earthly journey and at some point in your life you will be called to go within and reunite with your Inner Child. Relationship breakdown due to a lack of intimacy is the end result of a neglected and unloved Inner Child. The Divine Mind Conversation will teach you how to parent your Inner Child with the love and nurturing it needs so you can fully release the emotional chains of your past and spiral up above the line.

Today's Higher Idea: Your Inner Child is here to remind you to have a sense of humour and to stop taking life so seriously. Do whatever it takes to bring more laughter and joy into your life. Allow yourself to feel vulnerable. Go outside and spend a day playing.

Higher Idea #40 Be the Love that You Are

We have programmed ourselves to criticize others instead of uplifting them. We have been programmed to create separation instead of connection. For these destructive patterns to disappear, we are being called to remember our Forgotten Angels. We are being called to remember that love is at the core of who we are and to do whatever it takes to express love from that part of ourselves.

You may crave love and yearn to be loved, yet if your Fallen Angels are in control, the moment you experience even a glimpse of love, they are programmed to shut you down. Your Fallen Angels will communicate to you through your thoughts, which will affect how you feel and, therefore, affect how you act over the smallest of issues. If you do not know how to control the energy that is moving through you, they will direct you to close up, be afraid to feel, or stop you from receiving and giving love. Your inner Fallen Angel voices may then tell you to run away, to fight, to escape, or to move on. Do not listen! Instead do whatever it takes to break open to love. Drop into vulnerability and talk about your fear, let your tears be released, breathe and SIT IN the energy that is moving through your body. This energy will pass and harmony can be restored in moments. It is your choice.

When you transcend the ego or Fearful self, you let go of the idea that you are the center of the universe and everything revolves around you. Once you have released your ego from controlling your life, you are able to drop down from living in the head to living in the heart. This means you can come home from work and actually be fully present and engaged with your beloved and family. When you are being the love that you are, you can make eye contact, listen to what is being said without judgment and keep your tone of voice to a welcoming level. When you know that you are energetically connected to everyone, you will be less likely to harm another. Higher knowledge is remembering that any inner pain you project outside of yourself is guaranteed to boomerang back, causing your energy vibration to drop.

To live in the Freedom Frequency, you will be required to fully define the man or woman you want to be. Relationships offer the most powerful growth opportunity to deepen into love for yourself and to understand what it means to be *love* in action. Any relationship—whether it is with your parents, your beloved, your siblings, or your friends—will offer a time and space for you to discover and express your Loving Self, your Cruel self, your Angry self, your Happy Self, and so on. Everyone you relate to will mirror an aspect of you, showing you what *Selves* still require your attention. Can you be the first one who steps into love? Can you be the first one to apologize, or the first one to give a hug, or the first one to admit you misunderstood?

You can save yourself much grief and experience a drama free and stress free life by learning to connect with your heart intelligence. When you are open to learning from others, your heart is open. When you are not open to learning about yourself, you are vibrating at a lower frequency and your heart remains guarded. Remember, love cannot be taken away. Love does not cause pain. Love does not cause the heart to ache. Only the lack of love can cause pain and heartache.

Start today and connect with your Loving Self. Once you have an appreciation for who you are and can see others for who they truly are, you connect with the vibrations of love, the unified field that links you to the blueprint of your destiny. Now you can focus your attention on creating value in your life and sharing your soul inspired talents with the world. Life will support you in the most incredible and magical ways.

Love is the glue that binds everything together in physical reality. I suggest you put your focus on the vibration of love for everything you want manifested.

Today's Higher Idea: What if you discovered that *you* are the love you seek? Close your eyes and breathe the energy of love into your chest. As you exhale, breathe out love energy to all who are open to receiving it. Do this ten times slowly and with intention. Do you feel expansive, unlimited, and connected?

Higher Idea #41 Breaking Down the Heart-Wall

With all the tragedy on the planet, we may well wonder, *How can the Universe be a loving place?* Tragedy occurs when people walk through life with a closed or guarded heart. Love is the most powerful force, and if you are not willing to express love, life seems to have a way of orchestrating events that break our hearts open to *feeling*. Why do we need an illness, an accident, or a death in the family to break down the walls of separation and force everyone together to forgive and open his or her hearts?

Everyone has an energetic *heart-wall* whether we are aware of it or not. The *heart-wall* was created to protect you from hurt and pain when you were young, but now it can be the root cause of what holds you back from achieving your dreams or experiencing a fulfilling relationship.

I became aware of my *heart-wall* when I had a direct experience of the Divine twenty years ago. I had no idea up until that point that a heart-wall even existed, however; when I was shown this energetic wall wrapped tightly around my heart, which was an accumulation of layers upon layers of dark energy (trapped negative emotions) I knew my deepest purpose in the moment was to do whatever it took to dissolve these layers so I could experience the power of *enlightened love* in my life.

Today this information about the *heart-wall* has been scientifically proven. Dr. Bradley Nelson, a renowned holistic physician and author of *The Emotion Code*, reveals how emotionally-charged events from your past can still be haunting you in the form of "trapped emotions" around the heart.

Love cannot be taught, bought, borrowed, or stolen. Love can only be felt through an open heart. When your heart is open, you resonate with the higher vibrations of love, health, joy and prosperity. Love is a responsibility that teaches us the *ability to respond* to life instead of reacting. Responsibility is learning to become aware of your inner power and to recognize when you are either exerting your power over others or giving it away. When you allow others to trigger lower energies, such as anger or hate, you are giving up your power. Your power is in being kind, respectful, and keeping your heart open no matter what.

Your heart closes because you feel separate from others, yourself, or life. Your heart opens when you have loving thoughts about others and especially about yourself. Remembering to reclaim, embrace, and love the many Fallen and Forgotten Angels that are alive inside of you, is a powerful way to dissolve the *heart-wall*. Each Fallen Angel is linked to a perceived negative emotion and the more you allow yourself to feel and release these trapped layers of heavy energy, the more *life-force* energy can fill your heart dissolving all hurt and pain.

Meditation and deep breathing are a beautiful way to open your heart to yourself. Opening your heart is a choice you can make right now. You can choose to say, "I am remembering to love myself. I now choose to love and appreciate my heart's intelligence. I know I am safe and I now choose to trust myself. I now choose to live a heart-centered life."

When your brilliant heart is open, your natural gifts and talents unfold and creativity manifests. Allow yourself to become vulnerable. Through this state of openness, your mind and heart become one and you expand to a higher level of consciousness which will dramatically change your life for the better.

Today's Higher Idea: A beautiful daily practice is to ask your inner guides and teachers of love and light, who vibrate in the spiritual dimension, for assistance. You can say, "By Divine intention, I ask my Brilliant Self to assist in opening my heart and dissolving my heart-wall with ease and grace. I now choose to let go of my fear of loving others. I now make a conscious choice to be the love I AM. I now choose to love myself and trust life. I now choose to see that the universe supports me. And so it is."

Higher Idea #42 Love Your Body

Have you ever heard someone with low self-esteem say, *"I am just a human being?"* Starting today, I suggest you see yourself as a *brilliant human being*. Remember, your physical body is the temple that houses your soul. You are here to take care of this Divine temple so you can experience all the richness of life. You are now being asked to release the story of being wounded, damaged, and frail. As long as you keep repeating and believing in these lower ideas, you will remain in a cycle of weakness.

Through alternative medicine, energy work and infusing my body with the higher vibrations of love in the form of sound, color and light, I was able to heal my body of chronic back pain, fatigue, IBS, depression, allergies and transmuted ovarian cancer cells. I believe our body is so intelligent that it *knows* how to heal itself. In fact, the physical body is so intelligent that it can often produce substances similar to the drugs prescribed by a doctor. For example, when our mind is calm and peaceful, our body will produce a state similar to Valium. The vibrations within the Freedom Frequency will bring forth a profound state of love similar to the drug Ecstasy. We're all capable of producing these natural states that bring forth feelings of incredible peace, comfort, and love, and without the disastrous side effects.

Where love does not exist, illness makes a home. I am not sure where I read these words of profound truth, but these simple words have inspired me to learn how to love my body and to open my heart to who I am as a woman. Through the expansion of self-love, I began to understand and accept the direction in which my life was moving. Hating or disliking any part of my body allowed my body to remain in its ugly state because its ugly state was all I could see. As I began to love every part of my body, my body began to transform into the body I had always dreamed of having—naturally.

The worlds of health, wellness and longevity are available to you. If these worlds are important to you, then begin at once to let go of the diseased and frail ideas you have about yourself. I highly recommend you release the words *illness, weak, frail, wounded, kill,* and *damaged* from your vocabulary and replace them with new, empowering statements such as: "I am feeling incredible strength within my body," or "I now release my wounded stories," or "My body vibrates in total health." You'll be amazed by how your body changes when you focus on the health template that is already imprinted in your cells. Remember, thoughts have the power to create illness or a higher vibration of health in your body. What you focus on expands, so think higher thoughts and you'll experience a journey to new worlds you never knew existed.

Health is your natural state. Connecting to your Healthy Self will bring the energy vibrations of optimal health into every cell of your body. When you feel ill, you're vibrating in the frequency of fear. At that point, it's important to do whatever it takes to change your focus and spiral up in your thoughts, words, and actions. Express loving words such as "I love you body. I am sorry. Please forgive me."

My suggestions are not intended to replace the services and advice of your physician. I am here to share higher knowledge that can completely change your world for the better. We live in a society that spoon-feeds drugs and supplements to us. Doctors who practice Western-style medicine have a great purpose, which is to assist those who live in the Frequency of Fear. Those who vibrate above the line are tuned into the truth that we are already whole and complete and there is nothing to heal. This is a journey, a transformative journey, which many people around the world are living today.

All I ask is that you do your research. Question everything. You're much stronger in mind, body, and spirit than you have been led to believe. Your body knows when you do not love it. It's time to recognize that your body is not just material flesh but energy made up of light vibrations. Light carries information and vibrates at a very high frequency. If your body is full of heavy, fear-based energies, it will block the light or life-force energy from rejuvenating the body to an optimal level of health.

I highly recommend an excellent book called *You Can Heal Your Life* by Louise L. Hay. In the book, Hay provides *The List*, an invaluable reference exploring the correlation between a disease and the probable psychological cause.

As a result of the spiritual coaching work I do, I've found that many illnesses we experience are rooted in our mental and emotional dimensions. Our thoughts have become weak and dysfunctional. When our mind and body do not relate to one another, this causes inner turmoil.

As long as an inner struggle is occurring between our body and mind, we will experience a lack of ease. The cure is to arrange and bring order to an otherwise chaotic state of mind. We must make every effort to build a relationship with our body that demands respect. We can no longer take our body for granted. We can let go of the idea that we need to have a man-made body and step into our power as a Divine *being*, loving the form we have been given by our Creator.

Today's Higher Ideas:

Raise your vibration through exercise. Your body wants to move. Learn to listen to the wisdom of your body. Your body is always speaking to you. The more you move your body, the more energy and mental clarity you have to handle life's challenges. When your legs want to run, they will tell you. When your body wants to stretch, you may be drawn to practice yoga. The key is in following through with your body's request. It knows what it needs. Exercise is an expression of self-love, *body love.*

Raise your vibration by eating high vibrational food. People who vibrate at a higher frequency only fuel themselves with high vibrational food because they love and respect their bodies. Low vibrational food, such as meat, processed or fast food, does not make you feel good after you have eaten it. High vibrational food, such as fruits and vegetables, makes you feel light and energized. Your body will never ask for fast or processed food. It is only the *ego, the fearful mind,* that asks to be filled with toxic energy. Commit today to becoming consciously aware of what you eat and how you feel after you eat. This is an important step in having the energy you need to live your beautiful life. David Wolfe is one of my favorite authors and I love listening to his presentations and videos regarding raw and super foods. (See Resource section)

Raise Your Vibration with Sound Therapy. Science and western medicine are finally validating what shamans have known for a millennium. The healing energy of sound vibrations such as tuning fork therapy, listening to Baroque, playing of crystal bowls, or any sound that harmonizes with the frequency of the heart, so that the physical body resonates in the health and wellness vibration.

You can tap into the power to transform your physical body and align with your optimal health template. After all, health is your natural state of being.

Higher Idea #43 The Power of Your Breath

The most important thing in life is your *breath*. Without breath, you would not exist for more than mere minutes. One of the most powerful tools for opening the heart to love is learning how to breathe deeply. When you deepen your relationship with *breath,* you deepen into love.

Few individuals understand the importance of deep breathing. Breathing is life itself. When you are consciously breathing you know you are breathing much more than "just air". You are actually breathing in the same Source energy, life-force energy that creates universes. Prana or life-force energy feeds the mind, body, and soul; it is the connection to eternal health. We have become shallow breathers, but it's time to become one with the life-force energy that fills our bodies and breathe deeply into our belly.

Proper breathing from the diaphragm, cycling through the heart and all the energy centers within the body, can increase your capacity to discharge toxic energy. Deep breathing worked miracles for me in helping me to transform my dis-ease into a body that moved through life with ease.

Deep conscious breathing is when you are fully aware of each breath. You feel it. You embrace it. The benefits of deep-belly breathing are:

- Assists in releasing fear energies
- Brings more oxygen into the body
- Deepens your sexual expression
- Improves concentration
- Reduces stress and revitalizes your body
- Brings you into the present moment
- Deepens the communication between mind, body, and soul
- Integrates your spiritual, mental, emotional, and physical selves

Today's Higher Idea: Practice Higher Idea #44 on the next page.

Higher Idea #44 Your Daily Deep Breathing Practice

Following are a few simple steps you can take whenever you feel stressed or anxious. Deep belly breathing will instantly calm your mind and bring the higher vibrations of relaxation.

- Find a private place where you know you will not be disturbed. Outside in nature is perfect.

- Sit in a comfortable chair with your back straight. Close your eyes. Now take a deep, slow five-second breath in through your nose and take it all the way down into your belly. Then exhale for the same length of time through your nose.

- As soon as you have exhaled, take another breath and count to five again. Keep each breath naturally connected to the one before it. Do not pause between inhalation and exhalation.

- Now that you are comfortable breathing this way, visualize Prana (life-force) as a gold light entering your nostrils with each breath you inhale. Visualize a wave of this colored light spiraling down into all the parts of your body that feel tight and tense. Keep your focus on your breath as you now intentionally bring this life force energy into your heart center filling this area with love.

- Now bring the breath slowly down into your belly and allow this energy to expand into all your organs. Each inhalation and exhalation is a cycle. With each cycle, inhale in the energy of health, then exhale dis-ease, inhale peace, exhale stress, inhale love, exhale fear. With every exhale you are releasing this energy from your body and sending it back to Source. Cycle through ten times or until you feel a shift in your energy.

- Now you're ready to face the world once again.

Deep conscious breathing gives you more energy, greater mental clarity, and a higher level of trust in yourself.

Today's Higher Idea: When you feel stress or frustration building, practice deep-belly breathing.

Higher Idea #45 Breathe in Compassion

The first step in cultivating compassion is to have empathy for others. We all have the power to create heaven on earth when we breathe in the energy of compassion and send it out through our hearts to those who are suffering.

If your aim in life is to be happy, then become a compassionate person. Many people lack compassion and empathy for others because their hearts are closed to the giving and receiving of love. If we are self-centered, we only focus on our own needs and ignore the needs of others.

Having sympathy for someone is very different than having compassion. Sympathy means feeling sorry for others, which causes you to become caught in the emotional entangled energies of the one who suffers. You are not here to take on other people's energy. You are here to dive into your own Suffering self and as you do, you automatically tap into the vibration of the collective consciousness of all who suffer. As you dissolve the suffering seed within yourself, through the assistance of your own Compassionate Self, you contribute to the evolution of humanity. This is how important you are. Remember, we are all energetically connected.

This inner work allows you to tune into how others must feel in times of deep despair, sadness, and loneliness. This understanding will empower you to see the reason for the behavior of those who have mistreated you. As you learn to have more compassion for yourself, you will begin to have more compassion for others. Now you can hold space for others, through listening and being present to their needs.

Breathe in the energy of compassion that is already you. Compassion happens when you live with an open heart. When you are open, you have no reason to fear anything. Compassion brings forth the energy of togetherness without sympathy or feeling sorry for others. Compassionate detachment allows you to love others from a distance so they may evolve at their own pace.

Today's Higher Idea: Practice compassion, love, and kindness every day to inspire others to see beyond their suffering. We are not here to stay in our Suffering self. We are here to remember that we are more powerful than the pain we have experienced.

Higher Idea #46 Breathe in Gratitude

After you have crossed the bridge of Forgiveness, the vibration of Gratitude will open the gates to fully living in the Freedom Frequency. The vibration of gratitude will instantly create positive shifts in your life. When you choose to see the gifts in every moment and be grateful for the life lessons people bring, you are living above the line.

Some people take for granted the good that is already present in their lives. If you've already brought forth a practice of gratitude into your life—in which you acknowledge and are thankful for everything you receive, no matter what it is—then you have transformed a powerful Forgotten Angel into a Remembered Angel.

We have so much for which to be grateful. Look at the amazing planet we live on. The energy of gratitude has the power to shift your perspective completely and to pop you out of a fearful mind. Anytime you are in the pit of fear or have lost your faith in the Universe, ask the question, "What am I grateful for?" Continue to reflect on this question until you receive an answer.

Showing others how grateful you are for their kindness, generosity, time, or energy is important. You can uplift someone and change her or his state of mind instantly by just looking her/him in the eye, saying, "Thank you," and letting her/him know three reasons why you're grateful for having her/him in your life. This is one of the biggest gifts that we can give our loved ones, coworkers, family, or friends.

Today's Higher Idea: The gratitude vibration will spiral you up into the Freedom Frequency faster than you can say, "I am living above the line." Write in your journal about ten things for which you are grateful, and then share them with the ones you love. When faced with adversity ask, "How can I benefit from this?" or "What am I to learn from this?"

Higher Idea #47 Learn to Hold Space for Others

Did you know that you have the ability to stand in the fire of another's anger and not be affected by it in a negative way? I am not saying you must tolerate negative behavior—just that you don't have to let it affect you. Ultimately, self-love is not allowing the behavior of others to take away the love and peace that is you.

If you have attended any workshops you will know that "holding space" is the ability to sit in the energy of someone's anger, sadness, or fear while remaining calm, centered, and compassionately detached. Holding space is the art of being an observer or witness to another as they shift in consciousness and experience the gift that vulnerability brings. When you hold space for another, that person feels safe and supported; she or he trusts you completely because she/he knows you will not judge, which opens her/him up to expressing her/his deepest truth. Now the person can talk about whatever mess she/he has created, share her/his deep emotional pain and discover her/his own capacity to solve problems.

The most powerful resolution to conflict is showing appreciation for the Divine nature within the person before you. You know and trust that the person is not her or his anger; they are only transforming their inner dimensions. This person is living unconsciously in fear, and we must have compassion for all those still living below the line. This is not to say we must tolerate abuse. Holding space means you are not contributing or engaging in the emotional pollution. While holding space, you remember that underneath all anger is sadness, and underneath all sadness is fear. Underneath fear are the person's Forgotten Angels, who have the power to spiral her/ him up above the line.

When you hold the energy of compassion and someone feels angry, you have the power to stand unaffected by the person's rage. It's a skill that can be learned. When you resonate in the Freedom Frequency you can see the projected negative energy move *around* you instead of *through* you.

Holding space allows people to open up, to feel and stabilize as they discover answers to their questions. You're not there to give advice or your opinion. You're only there to emit love from your heart and consciously listen to the journey of another. Developing your ability to *hold the space* in everyday life allows you to be sensitive and listen consciously to each person in your presence.

Holding space also means understanding that whatever a person is saying about how she or he feels about you or anything else is that person's truth, not yours. Her/His Fallen Angels are expressing themselves, and Fallen Angels love to blame. You're allowing an important process to take place as powerful energies are released from the person's physical body that would otherwise be harmful if kept suppressed.

Today's Higher Idea: The next time you experience someone arguing, take a moment and recognize the Divine light within her/him as she/he verbally releases toxic energy from her/his body. Practice observing others with curiosity and compassion; it is a powerful skill. If you practice this skill, you'll be able to stand in the midst of chaos and not be affected in a negative way by those around you. This takes time and patience, but peace within any situation can be truly experienced by anyone if the desire is there. Recognize the Goddess/God within you and others.

Higher Idea #48 Honor Mother Earth

We have explored how we relate to others and ourselves, but this chapter would not be complete if we did not explore our relationship with the Earth. Many of us walk, drive, and build our homes on this beautiful planet without realizing she is a conscious and living being. Without her life support system, we couldn't survive. We're interrelated and can no longer take the planet we live on for granted.

Mother Earth feeds, shades, gives us warmth, protects, and provides us with an abundance of natural resources. We need to remind ourselves to become consciously aware of the responsibility we have for conserving the natural world.

We all have a natural frequency that resonates with the Earth's, which is harmonic in nature. There are natural frequencies and man-made frequencies. Man-made frequencies such as microwaves, TVs, and computers create disharmony in the body. Mother Earth has a natural frequency that will immediately harmonize your frequency. Only when you are vibrating in harmony can you create a healthy body and a healthy life.

I suggest you surround yourself with the natural frequencies of the Earth as often as you can by walking in nature or meditating under trees, even if they're in your backyard. Simply acknowledge and show appreciation for the natural beauty that surrounds you.

In ancient times, prior to God-worship, there was a culture that honored the Earth. It was a time of the Goddess, when the feminine principle was cherished for its life-giving qualities. Feminine energy is rising again, and as men and women embrace these nurturing inner qualities, we can all ride the wave to *enlightened love*. Once we achieve internal appreciation, we learn to extend our appreciation to the external world. As we uplift our lives, we can teach our children to live by the same principles.

Mother Earth does not need saving, she knows how to take care of herself. She can cleanse herself any time. Our earth is multi-dimensional just like *you*. If there is any saving to be done, it is saving yourself. She has offered herself as a school for your learning. She needs to be respected. She is aware of those who love her and those who do not. If you make the time to connect and send love into the crystalline core of Mother Earth, she will make sure that you are always guided to a safe place in times of destruction. The next time you are walking in nature, take time to feel your connection to the water, trees, and life around you. Mother Earth is always listening. She is waiting to nurture you.

Some simple contributions we can all make to honor our beautiful planet include:

- Join, support, or create a conscious movement that expands our global and social responsibility.

- Invest only in products or companies that honor all of life.

- Use natural products instead of chemicals.

- Eat natural or organic foods instead of chemically sprayed foods.

- Use natural fertilizers.

- Take part in an Earth Ceremony of Appreciation or global meditation.

- Send loving thoughts to the crystalline core of Mother Earth when you meditate.

- Walk on the grass with bare feet as often as you can.

- Hug trees! They are much more than your physical eyes can see.

Native cultures recognize the spirit in all living things. Aboriginal peoples have always maintained a deep connection to the Earth. They have much to teach us when we are ready to listen. Let's remember our native ancestors, the ones who were here first, and listen to the beat of their drums. Let's unite with our native brothers and sisters of the Earth, with the aboriginal spirit that connects us in our vision quest for freedom.

Today's Higher Idea: Drop your ego and hug a tree.

Chapter Five
Express Your Truth

Are you afraid of expressing your curiosity, interests, or deepest desires? What about expressing your needs or wants? It's not uncommon for people to hold back self expression for fear of being judged, laughed at, or criticized. Many of us hold back our truths because we are afraid to express the deepest parts of ourselves. This fear can leave us feeling powerless and dissatisfied, and it can impair our ability to connect meaningfully with others in our business and personal lives.

This chapter will focus on ways of creating healthy self expression through the power of *relating*. The evolution of the Self involves reestablishing your relationship with the internal worlds of your mind, emotions, and spirituality and deepening your soul's interactions with others. Relationships are as much about valuing yourself as they are about reaching out and helping others.

Spirituality is a journey toward truth and aligning with Source energy. It is not about finding yourself as much as it is about remembering the truth of who you are. Expressing your truth can be uncomfortable at first; however, when you learn how to express your truth from a place of love, compassion, and appreciation for what *is*, the uncomfortable energy that moves through your body begins to shift into freedom.

Higher Idea #49 Live in Truth

We have collectively created a huge fear in looking at ourselves that we deny truth and will argue our right to live in limitation, pain and suffering. We have learned to deceive others and especially ourselves, through lifetimes of observation and learned behavior due to a world suffering with low self esteem or no sense of self.

How can you raise your vibration and live in the Freedom Frequency? The answer is simple: Truth! The more truth you bring into your life, the lighter you become. Lies are wrought with heavy energies, especially when we lie to ourselves. Many people are afraid of truth; however, it's the quality of truth that marks people who are spiritually wealthy and noble. Truth allows us to open our eyes, remove the veil of denial, and untangle the illusions of our life.

The lack of truth has consequences. Lies are like scissors that cut away the attraction cords of any relationship, be it business or personal. Every act that is not built on truth will lead to self-sabotage. When you are vibrating in truth, you can no longer speak lies or manipulate others.

Truth asks you to get real with *what is so*. The journey toward truth means acknowledging and feeling any untruths hidden within your mind. The way to freedom is by moving through the frequency of fear so you can make the distinctions between what is illusion (lies we tell ourselves) and what is truth.

To create a world where love, trust and intimacy blossom we are being called to end the deception within our own homes. We no longer need to impress people or misrepresent our life in order to look good. Authenticity is sexy, it is cool, it is hip and it is the new truth. You can learn to tell the truth with an air of ease and grace. As you make the choice to express yourself authentically, you bring forth personal freedom. Reclaim your power by making a choice to live in truth.

Today's Higher Idea: What truths are you ready to express? The truth about how you feel in your relationship or how you feel about the path you are on? Identify with your Pretender self (we all have one) and tune into whether this self is in control of your life. Are you living a lie? How often do you lie to yourself and others? Who are you pretending to be? Observe without judgment. Be kind to yourself as new insights surface.

Higher Idea #50 Rise Up from Conflict

One of the most powerful books I have read was, Nonviolent Communication by Marshall B Rosenberg. He shows us how to express our feelings and needs from a giving heart, and connect to our compassionate nature when communicating.

Many of us have not been taught how to express what we feel or need and therefore fall into old behavior patterns often mimicking the dysfunctional way our parents related to each other.

Conflict in your outer world is a reflection of conflict within your own mind. The conflict between the ego and your soul is the only battle that creates hell in any and all relationships. When you are afraid of conflict you are afraid to face your own mind, your own Fallen Angels who interpret others and life experiences as wrong and bad.

When you are in conflict you are in your head and you are being asked to drop down into your heart and into your body and *feel* the energy that is alive inside of you. Conflict has a way of revealing the truth of where you are mentally, emotionally, and spiritually.

The root of conflict is *fear*—fear of being threatened, not being appreciated, understood, valued or acknowledged for the person you believe you are. If you have conflict in your relationships whether personal or professional, it means you are afraid of each other. If you are afraid of each other, you are also afraid of yourself. This is not love.

One of the biggest fears related to conflict is the *fear of being seen.* Being seen for all your perceived mistakes or failures, being seen in your vulnerability, your shame, guilt, or being found out that you have been pretending to be someone you are not. Fear of being seen brings forth the fear of being found out for not being as educated as others, for the wrongful acts of our past, or for not being as strong as you may pretend to be.

Today's Higher Idea: If we are to rise up out of conflict this requires us to stop being afraid of our emotions, of each other and embrace our own vulnerability. You are being called to communicate from a deeper place. Say to out loud, "I now choose to release my fear of conflict. I now choose to have a learning attitude about myself and others."

Higher Idea #51 Cultivating the Right Attitude

Are you a complainer? When you complain or have a negative attitude about life, you are really complaining about what you have created and your inability to cope with it. Buddhist philosophy identifies eight signposts to freedom. One signpost is *right* attitude or thought, which means to become consciously aware of your thoughts and start thinking from the highest point of view. When you complain, you have been feeding your mind garbage. What good does this do you?

Your attitude is important, and having a right attitude means releasing the garbage in the mind. When you move out of the realm of "I can't" to the realm of "I can" you are releasing the inner Fallen Angel that is saying, "I won't." Your mind will create resistance to thinking higher thoughts about your experience because it has been programmed to disapprove of yourself and others.

Your Divine intelligence breathes in the positive essence of your creations as you move out of the worlds of right, wrong, good, or bad into accepting the neutrality of life's Divine order. Happiness lives inside of you and you can choose to connect to this higher vibration even if your bills are not being paid or when you are not getting what you want. Complaining robs you of your happiness.

We are all capable of moving through suffering and pain by releasing the negative energetic charge we have associated with certain moments. You'll know you've transformed the emotional body when you can say, "I now choose to approve of myself and others and live above the line in the Freedom Frequency of life." With this attitude, you will be able to look back on your past with a smile and create heaven in your life.

Choose today to have an optimistic view about life. To have an attitude of knowing that things are going to turn around. To believe that this present moment is a blessing in disguise. To see that this is just a moment within a trillion moments of your life and you are preparing yourself to live in the freedom frequency of life.

Today's Higher Idea: Share with someone you love and express the words, "I have a learning attitude."

Higher Idea #52 Spiral Up in Your Thoughts

There is nothing that limits you or keeps you in a state of doubt except your thoughts. Your mental power is highly creative. You are either operating from a fear-based mind or your Divine Mind. Thoughts can either destroy or uplift you. Everything you taste, touch, feel, or smell was first created in your mind through thought. Your thoughts are often expressed through the words you speak, and if you believe what you say is true, then the energy behind your words will cause you to act.

Many people walk the same path every day doing habitual things but expecting their lives to change. For change to occur in your outer world, you must first *think and feel the change* in your inner world. Whatever you focus your thoughts on is what you will experience, whether you like it or not. When you recognize that it's the subconscious mind that dictates your experiences, you realize how important it is to understand and restructure the controlling thoughts that are manifesting the world you see.

Much of the time we're unaware that the thoughts we have are actually images. If I told you not to think about a red Lamborghini, (this is my inner Race Car Driver speaking) what would happen? Your mind would immediately picture a red Lamborghini. These pictures run through the mind at the speed of light, and it's only when we become consciously aware of our mental realm that we discover the inner movies we create.

You may appear outwardly nice to people, but what thoughts do you have when their backs are turned? Remember, we are all energetically connected. If people are spiritually attuned, they can also read your energy vibrations and the truth behind your words. How you feel about someone doesn't have to be expressed verbally for a person to know your vibration. Thoughts alone are easy to read when you have awareness. How you truly think about people will eventually make itself known and you will experience the effects of that thinking. Are you sending out loving and compassionate thoughts or hateful or envious thoughts?

It is good practice to be aware of your thoughts regarding others, but especially, to be aware of how you think about yourself. Negative thoughts about the self or others such as, "I don't deserve to be loved" or "He's a loser" are destructive. The thoughts you have about others mirror exactly how you feel about yourself. Any fear-based thoughts cannot continue if you want a better life. If you think too much, you cut yourself off from connecting to your heart. Less thinking and more feeling is the key.

When life is challenging, you may experience setbacks and delays in making your dreams come true. You may lose faith in yourself or question the journey you are on. Your doubt can become overwhelming. Your fear-ridden mind can take you on a wild and uncomfortable ride. Thoughts like "I can't do this," or "What was I thinking?" or "I'm not smart enough" can tend to cloud your better judgment. When you are in fear-based mind you doubt your capabilities, talents, and skills. This doesn't sound like fun, does it? Time to spiral UP and make a different choice on how you choose to think.

Your thoughts will become conflicting when you consciously or unconsciously surround yourself with negative images every day. These images enter your mind through television, music, movies, and even reading the newspaper. Your thoughts are energetic, so it's important to reduce the amount of negativity in your life by making a conscious choice and asking yourself, "Is what I'm doing now going to benefit my life?" If what you're doing doesn't make you a better person, then why bother? Find something that will expand your mind and uplift your life.

You create reality by what you choose to think and what you choose to believe in. That's how powerful your thinking is. You can have either fearful thoughts or freedom thoughts. The more aware you are of what you're thinking in the present moment, the more choice you have to change your thoughts and how you feel about your life.

Today's Higher Idea: You have a choice on which mind you want to operate from – Fear-based mind or your Divine Mind. To connect to your Divine Mind and uplift your mood, listen to Baroque music. The vibration of Baroque music stimulates whole brain thinking, enhances creativity, and at the same time, calms the mind.

Higher Idea #53 Spiral Up in Your Words

Do words have the power to affect your health and well-being? The answer is: Yes. Words have a lot of energy behind them, and they can affect you positively or negatively. Words are sound vibrations and they carry either a positive or negative charge which is fueled by your intention or the emotional energy you associate with the word. For instance, the word *love* carries a high frequency and has the power to heal and transmute all negativity, yet if you have fear associated with the word love, you will create a barrier to experiencing the profound freedom *love* brings.

Dr. Masaru Emoto, a Japanese visionary, researcher, and the author of *The Hidden Messages in Water*, (see Resources section) provided evidence that human thoughts and words affect the molecular structure of water. Water crystals exposed to verbal insults produced black and distorted water crystals. Water crystals exposed to loving and compassionate thoughts and words produced beautiful crystal configurations. Dr. Emoto has shown us through his extraordinary work that water takes on the energy vibrations of the environment. Since our physical bodies are made of 70 percent water, we are affected in the same way. Loving, encouraging, compassionate words produce harmonic energy in our bodies. Insults, negativity, and listening to harsh music produce disharmonic energy and will lower your vibration.

It's important to become aware of the words you speak and the words to which you listen. It is also important to become clear about the intent or motivation behind those words. Are they driven by ego, which is fear-based, or are you expressing yourself from the heart, from a caring perspective? One word or term expressed repeatedly with negative intention can manifest dire consequences. The Law of Attraction states that whatever you focus on, you create more of in the physical realm. For example, there is currently so much discussion about breast cancer in the world that women are experiencing an alarming increase in the manifestation of it. We have given this word so much power. What if the cure were as simple as becoming aware of our own inner Cancer self, the Fallen Angel that knows it is not loved? What if we collectively held space and connected to our Cancer selves and dissolved the seed within that carries the negative energetic charge? Now we can say, "I now take my power back." If we can dissolve anger, dissolve the disapproval, or any negative emotion completely with this process, then what if this higher idea could dissolve dis-ease, the lack of ease in the body? Can we dissolve the negative charge of this word, the word *cancer,* and release the fear associated with it? As long as we have fear wrapped around the word, we will create the exact thing we don't want. I believe *self-love* can cure anything, especially when it has been proven that loving thoughts and words have the power to heal and create inner beauty. Now we can let our wings expand and see that heaven is right here, right now.

If you speak with the intent to manipulate, judge, criticize, or deceive others, you will experience the results of those words. If you are ever having a bad day, check your state of mind to see whether you have projected any negativity toward anyone. What's coming back to you is a result of your own thinking. Remember, you get back what you put out. In order to experience a transformation in your mental dimensions, you must change your idea of what communication is. You can use words either to help you in the creation process or as destructive weapons that will boomerang right back at you. The choice is yours.

Today's Higher Idea: The vibration of your words can either spiral you down toward destruction or spiral you up to living above the line. If you are ready to raise your vibration and live in the Freedom Frequency, start today and spiral up in your *word* by practicing the following higher expressions.

- I am grateful for everything in my life.
- I am living with ease and grace.
- I love and appreciate myself as I am.
- The more I love myself, the more love I have to give others.
- I am now attracting loving and meaningful relationships.
- I love my soul-inspiring business, and I am richly rewarded creatively and financially.
- I always communicate clearly and effectively.
- I am always in the right place at the right time.
- This is an abundant universe and there is plenty for all.
- I am prosperous, and I share my wealth with others.
- I always make time to play and enjoy myself.
- I recognize time is fluid, and I have plenty of time for everything.

And So It Is!

Higher Idea #54 Spiral Up in Your Actions

Do you ever question the motivation behind your actions? Are you doing things to make yourself look good, or are you actually assisting others to achieve their dreams?

Thought is the first level of creation. It's followed by feelings, which we express in both words and actions. Everything you say is an expression of thought or feeling with action following. You can talk all you want about love; it will be your actions that will be the true expression of your heart.

You are either taking action from one of two realms of consciousness – fear-based action or soul-inspired action. Fear-based actions are when you allow ego to dominate, like approaching a situation from a place of control, greed or seeking revenge because you believe someone did you wrong. If you take action from a place of fear, need or desperation you are not in alignment with freedom. Instead, you'll experience the consequences of those fear-based actions.

To shift into higher vibrations of freedom, I suggest only take inspired action. At the core of inspired action is spirit, your Divine Mind. When you take action from this place your results are always rewarding and deeply fulfilling.

Recognize the power behind your thoughts, words, and actions. If you lie, others will be deceitful with you. If you cheat others, someone else will cheat you. If you hate, you will only see a hateful world and you will draw that negative energy to yourself, all the while wondering why things seem to be going wrong. That's how powerful you truly are. Whatever you think and believe is what you experience. Every cause has an effect, and every choice has consequences you must face.

Today's Higher Idea: Expand your awareness of every action you take, and then connect to your Observer Self. Can you rewind the movie of your life and identify where you took fear-based action and when you took inspired action? Observe yourself without judgment.

96

Higher Idea #55 See People as Divine Messengers

I believe every person is playing a role in your life for a higher purpose. You are the creator of your life and have attracted every person for a reason. You will meet many people who are Divine messengers. These beautiful souls will create tremendous and painful acts just to remind you to *feel* again, to open your heart again, and to remind you to connect with your Fallen Angels so they can be released and integrated into light.

People and circumstances seem miraculously to appear just at the right moment to teach you who you are, how you are thinking, and what you believe. You've created everyone to assist you with the choices you have made. If you choose to learn about love, you may attract people who are not loving so you can learn how to be compassionate and understanding and to embody forgiveness. If you want to attract a man who loves and accepts you for who you are, you may have to go through a few relationships to prepare you mentally, emotionally, and spiritually. Every event and circumstance offers a powerful learning opportunity.

The parents who may not show love, the boss who is unappreciative, the men who use or abuse you or the women who disrespect you—they're all there to remind you of where you are vibrating and to show you how much you are not loving or respecting yourself. Learn to see everyone as an angel in disguise and listen to her or his message of truth. Everyone is here to empower you to let go of who you are *not* so you can embrace who you are.

If you're not enjoying where you are in life, it's up to you to change it. You may start by asking yourself the question, "How did I get myself here?" Every experience happens for a reason, yet we often don't realize this until later in life.

Everyone you meet is a Divine messenger, an *earth angel,* who is reminding you of why you came to this planet in the first place. Relating to others with a high willingness to learn, you can then explore issues with a greater understanding of everyone present. When you see others as angels in your life, you are less likely to create conflict.

Today's Higher Idea: See everyone you meet as an *earth angel* who is here to give you a message and remind you of where you are vibrating in life. Everyone is a mirror reflection of you.

97

Higher Idea #56 Heart to Heart Communication

Heart to heart communication is a wonderful way to practice raising your vibration and infusing love in any relationship. Here, you have an opportunity to learn how to respond to others instead of reacting or blaming. Underneath all conflict is a need to be heard, to be appreciated, and to be understood.

Heart to heart communication is a great practice, especially if a relationship is in a power struggle phase. If you believe you are losing your identity, your inner Fallen Angels will create separation via blame and focus on the flaws or faults in your partner. If your partner doesn't change into the person you want him/her to be, you may feel frustrated because your efforts to "improve" him/her aren't appreciated. Any form of conversation from this state of mind may generate a sense of failure that may cause you to start putting up walls of resistance. This is an unconscious relationship pattern and will only transform into something meaningful when each person becomes personally accountable for how she/he feels and responsible for her/his own actions and behaviors.

Heart to heart communication offers each person an opportunity to express herself/himself eye to eye, face to face, and soul to soul. There are no demands, only requests. You begin statements with, "I am feeling...What I am afraid of is...What makes me feel this way is...My life lesson is...What I appreciate about you is...What I am thankful for is..."

By sharing how you feel and admitting that your unloving actions or behaviors originate from a place of fear and no longer serve the relationship, you open yourself up to having an authentic conversation. There is no blame, guilt, or judgment here because you see how you contributed to the situation for your own evolution of Self.

Heart to heart communication is about getting out of the head (thinking) and being fully present (in your body) with the one sitting across from you. When you offer direct eye contact and choose to observe without judgment, you can truly see that underneath all perceived negative emotions and fear, there sits a Divine human being. How blessed are you! When the other person feels heard, appreciated, and understood, her or his negative (fear-based) behavior begins to dissolve.

Conscious relationships are developed when you practice living from your heart and end the blame game. You no longer focus on changing your partner or pointing out faults. Instead, you focus on doing whatever it takes to empower each other. To empower yourself you will be asked to dissolve your own heart wall, raise your own vibration from fear to love, and have a learning attitude about your partner. This takes practice and patience, of course; however, your desire to evolve, live above the line, and live a heart-centered life will inspire you.

Heart to heart communication is about getting real with how you feel and what it is you need. Expressing your feelings can sometimes feel painful because you may be reminded of past failures, tragedies, or perceived wrongdoings. Do not allow any moment of life's experiences to keep you down. You are much greater than a *moment*. As you commit to spiraling out of the lower vibrations of energy and have dissolved the negative charge, life will open new doors of possibilities.

We can either have soulful moments or ego hours. The choice is yours. You will know when the ego has arrived when the voice in your head tells you how wrong or bad your spouse/partner are and you either want to fight or flee. A soul moment is when you can sit, breathe, and just BE with the sensenations in your body and express what you are afraid of. Your vulnerability is the gateway to self empowerment and enlightenment.

When you are open to listening and learning, you stop taking things personally. Hurtful words expressed reflect how that individual feels about herself/himself. They are never about you. The more you practice heart to heart communication, the more happiness and harmony you will bring into your relationships. You have the power to dissolve conflict and arguments completely.

Today's Higher Idea: Practice living from your heart by putting your hand on your heart and breathing into your heart for 5 minutes. Say to yourself, "I am releasing all fear wrapped around the idea of communicating my feelings and needs. I am now open to listening to the feelings and needs of my beloved." Remember, what you most want from others is sometimes the exact same thing you have not been able to give.

Higher Idea #57 Allow Others to Be Right

Is being *right* working for you? Having to be right all the time is a controlling behavior. It can lead to power struggles, which ultimately create walls of resistance between you and the people you love or respect.

Often, we get so caught up in our need to feel vindicated or understood that we take the long route to resolving conflict. Feuds can last for days or lifetimes when arguments could have been turned around in moments with compassion and understanding. When you let go of the belief that you need to defend, fight, or argue in order to be heard, you begin to spiral up into the realm of conscious relationships.

When you connect to your Divine Mind you become the observer instead of the one who judges self or another. When you seek to educate yourself and learn how to dive into conflict without taking anything personally you make a quantum leap in your evolution of Self. This is a journey and takes much practice.

People are in your life to challenge your Fallen Angels so you can become aware of how much control these inner selves have in your life. Rising up out of conflict, especially in intimate relationships, is having the courage to face your beloved, look her/him in the eye, and share how you *feel, express what you need and what you are afraid of.* Here you have the opportunity to step into agreement and see the soul, the divinity that stands before you. When someone agrees with you, how do you feel? Happy right? Exactly! You have the power to restore harmony and bring joy into people's lives with your kind words and kind action.

If you want to create deeper connections with your partner or loved ones, I suggest you seek agreement and allow others to be right. You can always find ways to agree on things. Allowing others to be right releases tension and stress and shows you have a learning attitude.

Today's Higher Idea: Having to be *right* takes up so much energy. If you are feeling exhausted maybe it is a sign to let go of your righteousness. You learn powerful life lessons in every relationship no matter whether a person is in our life for a reason, a season, or lifetime. Next time you are communicating, seek agreement. You can say, "I agree. You are absolutely right!"

Higher Idea #58 Create Soul Connections

Have you ever noticed that if you focus on how bad your relationship is, it just gets worse? The more negative attention you give anything, the more you create what you do not want. Your relationships will greatly improve if you choose to see your beloved or partner as a *soul* instead of a person you believe makes you mad or frustrated. When you focus on the things that make the relationship fulfilling, you will experience just that—a fulfilling relationship. Use your imagination and the power of your mind to visualize greater possibilities and positive outcomes. Instead of expecting the worst, first create the best possible scenario in your mind and then watch your relationships transform.

The goal when communicating with others is to *relate* rather than react. Relationships are an opportunity to seek understanding about yourself. If you feel you are not being understood, then you are being asked to communicate more effectively. You are being asked to go deeper into truth. When you make a conscious choice to stop the abusive pattern of yelling, shoving, swearing, or raising your voice at another you raise your vibration to that of self maturity and emotional mastery.

If you have painful experiences when communicating with your partner, family members, or other significant people in your life, then maybe it's time to ask yourself, "Do the feelings I have right now remind me of how I felt when I was a child? What's the lesson here?" Maybe it's time for you to say something kind and meaningful to those who trigger a negative energetic charge. Maybe your soul is calling you to step *first* into love. Surprise people with kindness such as a hug, an apology, or thoughtful words. You have the power to weaken all negative influences just by being kind, thoughtful, and loving. The key is to be open and honest about who you are and not to blame others for how you feel.

When you stop blaming others for how you feel or for a situation gone wrong, you will transform your relationship into something you have always wanted. Admit how you could have contributed to the problem at hand, and now focus on how you both can create a win-win. If an apology is required, apologize because you value your relationship more than your ego. This practice will help you to explore issues or problems honestly with knowledge, understanding, and love. On the other side of conflict is a wonderful gift awaiting you—an enriched relationship.

Releasing the fears surrounding communication allows for change. If an argument ensues, know that it is designed to bring forth clarity. The *Divine Mind Conversation* is a powerful technique that when practiced often can end an argument in five minutes. If two people are arguing for more than fifteen minutes, it means a Fallen Angel has taken over and they have become puppets on a string. Such an argument can only stop when the voice of soul love is heard from within. Every argument is actually a misunderstanding about two people's needs not being met.

When we learn to ask the right questions, let go of making assumptions, and allow for others' points of view to be expressed, we become empowered. Our energy sphere resonates in the world of understanding and compassion.

Mutual agreements must be made and followed through for future communications to be more harmonious. Issues that arise force us to find solutions that will help us evolve to the next level of being. The next time an issue is put on the table, take a deep breath and ask your Brilliant Self to give you the power to move through any uncomfortable situation. You'll experience moments of soul connection instead of two egos battling it out for hours to see who will win. The moment you realize your behavior is hurtful, embarrassing, or damaging to the people around you, you need to stop and do whatever it takes to get your thought vibrations above the line.

Never take out your rage on another human being or animal. If you need to yell, *yell at your Angry self,* for it is this *self* that carries the seed of your crisis. Releasing this energy will spiral you up into the Freedom Frequency. If you need to vent the uncomfortable energy in the Fear Frequency, redirect your energy to an inanimate object such as a couch or pillow. Kneeling down and beating up your couch or pillow instead of projecting it onto a loved one helps to vent frustration and allows for a much healthier release (see Resources section).

Taking responsibility for how you feel shows maturity and the determination to become a better person. Do not be afraid to address issues. Issues are the catalysts for correcting behavior patterns and releasing any fear that's holding you back from experiencing what you need or desire. Trust that you have the power to move through any problem or any challenge that life gives you.

If conflict gets out of control and you suffer emotional, mental, or physical abuse, you must ask yourself, "What action do I need to take to change my experience?" or "Who I am being that I allow this behavior to be in my life?" "How can I disengage and not contribute to this unhealthy cycle?" If someone is mean, rude, or constantly crushing your spirit, he/she is letting you know that it is time for you to gain your power back. Never stay where you're not appreciated. You always have a choice to seek others who will support and respect you rather than hurt or limit you.

Happiness within relationships comes from embracing, embodying, and nurturing the Happy Self. The more you and your partner make the relationship a priority, the more you create a soul connection. You create soul connections when you end the game of *being right* or blaming others for your own life experiences. Instead, you can lead by example by sharing the truth about your current vibration and what you want to experience in greater abundance. In this way, you tap into your own spiritual power and create each day in a vibration of appreciation and love.

Soul connections are created when you open up to higher self expression. The vibration of *pleasure* will allow a higher self expression of love for self and others to integrate much quicker. Anytime you practice saying positive statements, a higher idea is to bring the energy of *pleasure*, calmness, and sincerity into your expression. The more you do the inner work of creating a beautiful mind and expanding your heart, you begin to express new possibilities which will attract people into your life who want to support you in your cause.

Today's Higher Idea: Every day is a new day. Listen to your heart and connect to the heart of another. Make every effort to listen to others' points of view instead of making a judgment or creating wrongness. If you do not understand, seek to learn more.

Higher Idea #59 Upgrade Your Sphere of Influence

Do the people in your life inspire and encourage you to live above the line in the *Freedom Frequency*? Raising your vibration out of the worlds of suffering, pain, illness, or lack involves changing your environment, which may include changing some of the people with whom you associate.

If you're wondering why certain people are in your life, it's because your vibration resonates with their vibrations. If you want to attract different people into your life, you have the power to direct your vibrations to a higher frequency. Remember, successful people associate with other successful people and people who are passionate about life. If you want to learn how to become prosperous, you'll advance further if you associate with those who are prosperous. If you want more peace in your life, then I suggest you associate with those who have already obtained peace of mind.

Everyone you meet and connect with in life mirrors your state of mind. For example, your brain transmits thought vibrations that are picked up by others who are transmitting the same frequency. If you have low self-esteem, you only attract people with low self-esteem. As your state of mind spirals up, so do your relationships, and you may recognize that the people you once thought of as friends may not have your best interests at heart.

Your surroundings change the moment you project a cord of intention to a higher frequency in which you desire to vibrate. As you spiral up, you may find that many people in your present sphere may not be ready to leave the comfort zone of the frequency in which they vibrate. There is usually a grieving process as you let go of people who no longer support your journey. Setting others free with love is the most honoring way of ending any relationship. Remember, everyone is growing at her or his own pace.

Today's Higher Idea: Start connecting with people who talk about higher ideas instead of those who just talk about other people. When you have the courage to say goodbye and turn towards the direction of your dreams you will discover many amazing souls who want to say hi!

Chapter Six
Give Your Imagination a Purpose

Living above the line requires the application of one of your biggest gifts—*your imagination.* The power of your imagination can change your circumstances, your environment, attract wealth and meaningful relationships into your life, and improve your health dramatically. When you expand your awareness, direct your mental and emotional energy toward a greater reality, and transform your Forgotten Angels into Remembered Angels, you then align with the Creator within. Here you see yourself as whole, the complete You!

Unfortunately, as we move into adulthood, our imagination is often dormant. Learning to utilize this powerful gift, your *imagination*, will give you the power to transform your life.

This chapter will show you how your imagination is the gateway to your invisible worlds, your emotional, mental, and spiritual dimensions. I will show you how the vision you hold in your heart is what guides you to your destiny, the reason you are here on this planet in the first place. And I will show you that the best way to connect with your inner Fallen or Forgotten Angels is through the power of your imagination. Using your imagination, you can tap into internal forces that will give you the power to heal your body, overcome fear, change behavior patterns, and bring forth hidden talents. Your imagination opens the door to the inner worlds of your subconscious and Divine Mind, which will allow you to bring forth the power of insight, higher vision and creative expression.

Higher Idea #60 A Great Life Starts with a Vision

The vision of your life is not necessarily about creating a career or how you are going to make money. That will formulate as you gain clarity on the person you want to *BE*. What matters most is how you see yourself now and in the future. When you have the courage to redirect your focus from outside of yourself and explore your invisible worlds, which are very much *alive* inside of you, a whole new perspective on life begins to take shape.

The more clarity you have about who you want to *be* and how you want to live, the more ideas and opportunities you attract. If all you see is a void in your future, then you will experience just that—the *unknown*. So it would be a higher idea to project out your own prophecy that is filled with a grander vision for yourself and your family.

If you do not determine the path for yourself, then there is the possibility of being swept away into another person's reality, which may not be in alignment with your dreams and vision. Creating a vision will give you a strong enough focus and desire to prevent your unresolved Fallen Angels from discouraging you. Trust that once you have a vision of where you want to go, you will meet others along the path who have a similar vision of *freedom*.

Remember the forces of the universe are always with you. The only thing against you is your inner Fallen Angels, and it is your responsibility to go within and take your power back. Learning how to use your imagination in the right way is the most effective approach to releasing Fallen Angels with love and light. Then exchange each Fallen Angel with a Forgotten Angel (one that lives above the line) so that you remember your Divine power.

Your mind is vast and powerful, and when you learn how to direct its energies with your imagination and have them work for you rather than against you, you will be living in the Freedom Frequency of life. For instance, you may have the desire to travel or live in another country. Change can be overwhelming, but if you plan and organize your life with your imagination first, you can create the necessary steps and possible scenarios that create joy and attract infinite possibilities.

Now your *fearful mind* may take over and create visions of something *bad* happening to you in an attempt to pop that bubble of freedom. Trust that the images and higher visions coming to you are from spirit. Cancel all images that do not serve you or make you feel joyful. It is your Divine Mind that brings the joy and freedom you seek.

We are also on this earth to create a new vision for humanity. If we all collectively focus on a vision of connection, unity, and love for all, we have the power to birth a new reality. Our heart is calling for all of us to step into a higher vision and remember our deepest truth. The more clarity and insights you have about who you are and the power that resonates in every cell of your being, the more your vision expands, giving you the gift of freedom.

Today's Higher Idea: Visualize our beautiful planet ten years from now and how we are all experiencing heaven on earth. Infinite possibilities.

Higher Idea #61 Practice Creative Visualization

Have you ever felt so close to realizing your dream, and then for some reason, everything fell apart and now it seems as if you are at the exact opposite end of what you wanted to create? You will experience great resistance to change if your mind is constantly creating fearful mental images. Your Fallen Angels will resist everything you want until they are gently persuaded and come into agreement with what you desire. Your subconscious mind is here to serve you. Your subconscious mind has been programmed to live in the fear frequency, and now it is up to you to awaken to the power that is within.

Your heart and mind must come to agreement on whatever it is you desire. Since your Fallen Angels reside in your subconscious, and you cannot physically taste, touch, feel, hear or see your subconscious mind, wouldn't it make sense to use your imagination so you can? Creative visualization is a powerful tool you can use to connect with hidden parts of yourself.

Here are a few examples of how you can use the power of creative visualization to make you feel a greater sense of relief and empower you at the same time.

Can't Keep My Head Above Water—When you feel this way, visualize yourself in the water; you are exhausted and can barely keep your head above the water's surface. Now look down into the water and unplug the plug. See the water level going down until there is no more water. Now you realize you were in a bathtub. Feel the relief.

Feel Stuck in Life—When you feel this way, visualize yourself stuck in the mud. Now see yourself clutching onto a branch and pulling yourself out. See yourself standing on solid ground; take a deep breath and walk forward. Feel the freedom you have in moving forward with ease now.

Heavy Burden on Shoulders—When you feel this way, visualize yourself with a heavy backpack full of bricks. Now see yourself unhooking the backpack and letting it fall to the ground. Feel how much lighter you are. Take three slow deep belly breaths and exhale slowly.

Feeling Pressure—You may feel as if you have a vice grip on your head or someone is pushing down on you. Close your eyes and see yourself sitting on a chair with a vice grip on your head. See yourself releasing the vice grip and taking it off your head. Feel the release. This works!

If you feel someone is pushing you down, turn around and see who it is. Now take the person's hands off you and tell him or her that you are taking your power back.

Now you are using your imagination *for* you instead of against you. This is your Divine power.

Today's Higher Idea: Any time you are feeling stressed, take five minutes to state how you feel, using a metaphor, and then use your imagination to change the scene and empower yourself.

Higher Idea #62 Live Every Day with Intention

Are you experiencing instantaneous creations? Have you thought of someone and then next minute the person you were just thinking about calls you on the phone? Or you're thinking about going out for dinner to your favorite restaurant and then your beloved walks in the room and asks you if you would like to go out for dinner and they just happen to mention the name of your favorite restaurant? Or, when your thoughts are focused on how bad life is, you then stub your toe or the meeting you were looking forward to is canceled? Whatever you concentrate on will expand in your reality and this is why it is so important to become conscious of the thoughts you are projecting out.

Conscious or Divine intentions are defined as focused attention or giving direction to the mind on what it is you want to experience. A powerful way to tune into the *Creator* within, your Divine Mind, is to create Divine Intentions, which focus more on raising your vibration and help you clarify how you want to *feel* throughout the day. Everything you want to experience in life is based on how you want to *feel* within, such as more joy, love, respect or appreciation. Consciously creating an intention on how you want to *feel* during the day or week would be wise and therefore not reliant on an external outcome.

Since every day offers a new opportunity to show up and live the highest version of who you are, you can intentionally create how you want your day or week to unfold. A daily intention will direct the mind to what it is you want to create in order to experience *feel good* sensations in your body. For example, when you wake up each morning state out loud, "With Divine Intention, I now release all negative thought projections and consciously create my day to be one of ease and grace."

Every Sunday evening before you sleep, I suggest you also create a weekly intention to set up your week, such as "With Divine Intention, I now create my week to be full of energy, abundance of all good things, creative flow in my work and to be respected and appreciated by others." Visualize and feel the difference this intention can bring into your life.

Today's Higher Idea: Whenever you feel things are not working out, go to the place of your original intention to see if it was in alignment with your values, energy and beliefs. If not, start again and set a new intention that resonates from the heart.

Higher Idea #63 See Your Body in Optimal Health

You have access to transforming your physical body into a higher vibration of health. I believe that the power of a higher love and your imagination can transform all mental, emotional, and physical pain.

I suffered with chronic back pain for many years, and the only thing my doctors recommended at the time was a drug to numb the pain. Unfortunately, I was at a point where drugs were having no effect, so my doctor recommended back surgery. In that moment, my body signaled an alarm so loud I could not ignore it. I honor Western medicine and see the need for it in severe cases for those who vibrate below the line. However, I made the choice to seek answers in the opposite direction. I made the choice to find an alternative to healing my pain and to find a health care practitioner who did not believe drugs and/or surgery were the answers to every health issue. I was also ready to test the theory of mind power in healing my body.

I began to do light exercises every day such as walking or simple stretching. I was then drawn to meditation. For years, I would only meditate on a chair, but my intuition was guiding me to sit on the floor, which I found to be extremely uncomfortable. I realized how my meditation was giving birth to an active imagination, and my Brilliant Self continually reminded me to trust the process. I could not believe how afraid I was of my own mind, the fear of what I would find. My ego did not want me going within, so it created quite the inner drama game, putting up a huge amount of resistance. Thankfully, my devotion to my soul's calling was growing bigger than the fearful voices of my Fallen Angels, so I eventually made my way to the floor. Instead of fearing the pain, I began to breathe into it. Placing my full awareness on my back, my body began to show me deeper parts of myself of which I had been completely unaware. My pain took on a form as my mind's eye opened and I was shown an inner universe, my divine health blueprint, and how I could integrate with it.

I could see gold rings that were wrapped around what appeared to be long spaghetti-like cords. As my awareness expanded, I could see dozens of gold rings tightly holding these cords. I intuitively knew I was to cut them, so I instantly began cutting the gold rings with my imaginary scissors and WOW! I could feel the pain in my back instantly releasing. The relief I felt in that moment was profound, and then I began to cry uncontrollably. The emotional release was exactly what I needed, and once it was complete, I then imagined my body being filled with golden light, and I knew Divine intelligence was transforming that area of my body. Over the next few months, any time I felt pain in my back, I would simply close my eyes and cut the rings. The intensity of my chronic back pain began to decrease with every session until eventually it was completely gone.

With further insight, I realized that the rings had symbolized the unhealthy bond of the man I had been married to many years earlier. I had not realized how much resentment I had been carrying. Now I had cut myself free from a past that no longer served me.

I am happy to say that I no longer have any imaginary rings to cut and I have completely freed myself of chronic back pain and all the illnesses I described in this book's introduction. When you honor yourself, trust in your intuition and dare to take the journey into your subconscious mind, you will be shown the way to emotional, mental, spiritual, and physical freedom.

Pain reminds you that your body is in disharmony and you immediately need to change your course of action. You have extraordinary capabilities to dissolve pain and to transform your physical body through the power of your imagination. Connecting to your Divine Mind you integrate your health blueprint which activates cellular memory to remember the truth of who you are – Divine perfection.

Today's Higher Idea: Close your eyes and visualize a violet flame around your body as if you are standing in a purple bubble. You can say, "By divine intention, I now ask the violet flame to transmute all negative energy in and around my physical body. I now ask that my cellular blueprint be activated to that of divine perfection. Health is my natural state. And so it is."

Higher Idea #64 Practice Meditation

What excuse do you have that stops you from meditating? Is it, "I don't have time," or "I can't focus," or "I can't sit still," or "There are too many thoughts in my head"?

Why is it that we will sit behind the wheel of a vehicle and put ourselves into the chaos of traffic, but putting ourselves into the chaos of our thoughts is too scary? If we are afraid of our minds and ourselves, we then live in fear of others and the world we live in. One of the main reasons why I teach meditation is to assist people in relinquishing the fears that limits them so they can see that underneath all fear is their own divinity.

Meditation is the most transformative tool that I practice and teach. Every sage or prophet became such through the power of meditation. You embody what you constantly think about, so if you want to embody the higher vibrations within the Freedom Frequency, then I suggest meditation. In meditation, you become the observer of your thoughts instead of engaging in them. Meditation is about being. Meditation connects you to your Divine Mind and to all your Forgotten Angels that embody higher intelligence.

When you meditate, you enter the theta state. It is known that learning is accelerated when you are in a trance-like state. Meditation leads the way to whole brain thinking, integrating the activity of both left and right hemispheres. This integration opens the doors of perception, allowing higher information as well as higher forms of light to fill the mind, body, and soul. Becoming more mindful of your thoughts, words, and actions will inspire you toward a higher expression of character.

If you have time to watch a thirty-minute television show, you have time to meditate. There is no right or wrong way to meditate. If you feel resistance to meditation, it's because you're afraid to discover what's in your mind. Meditation will guide you to discover the secrets to overcoming your fear.

When you meditate for long periods of time, images will appear; sometimes a sequence of images, just like a movie, will cross the screen of your mind. These images are like billboards, offering you guidance on your journey. It is here you receive all the answers to your questions.

To manifest what you want in this world, you cannot just sit and wait for it. You need to take inspired action! Action includes physical and mental action, emotional responses, and spiritual disciplines that lead to a desired outcome. If you take action from a place of fear or are constantly pushing to make something happen, and you may be disappointed with your results.

Below is a simple guideline for people who are new to meditation. I highly recommend a silent meditation, which allows you to explore your thoughts. This meditation is not about quieting the mind—that takes greater practice. There is no goal here. Just sit and be. Take approximately fifteen minutes to do this exercise.

- Prepare the room by turning off the lights, phone, computer, and television.

- Light a candle.

- If you live with others, communicate your intentions so you will not be disturbed.

- Sit on a chair with feet flat on the floor.

- Relax your arms on the top of your thighs with palms facing up.

- Now close your eyes.

- Take three slow deep breaths in through your nose and release slowly again through your nose.

- Keep your focus on your breath.

- Observe your thoughts and sit in silence for fifteen minutes.

- If your thoughts become too overwhelming, say, "Thank you" to your thoughts and let them pass by. Return the focus to your breath.

- Sit and listen to the silence that's around you.

- Congratulations! You're meditating and on the way to transforming your mind, soul, body, and life.

Meditation is known to reduce stress, enhance concentration and heighten clarity in solving problems. For this reason, many business executives are tuning into the many benefits that meditation offers.

Leaders are known for making quick decisions. Enlightened leaders meditate first before making any decision. They let their Brilliant Self guide them in making the best possible choices that will serve everyone as they connect to their heart, values, and the principles that guide their lives. Whenever you are asked to make a decision, you can say, "I will meditate on the answer, and I will let you know my decision in 24 to 48 hours."

Today's Higher Idea: Practice the above meditation every evening to center yourself. You are the creator of your schedule, so it is important to take time for you and awaken to your spirituality.

Higher Idea #65 Dissolving the Pain

Once you practice this very powerful visualization technique, you can instantly dissolve headaches, migraines, back pain, and well, actually any pain. This technique does take practice, and it is not meant to replace your doctor. You can learn to release the energy of pain through any of your seven main energy centers, also known as *chakras*. These energy centers are like universal doorways to health as they receive, process and transmit universal energy. You actually have many energy centers in and around your physical body; however, for this exercise, let's just focus on one.

For example, if you have a headache, sit up straight and bring your full attention and awareness to the sixth chakra, your third eye area which is located between in the middle of your forehead. Close your eyes and surrender to your imagination. First give the pain or toxic energy inside your head a form (either a cloud of energy or a black oily blob of goo); it doesn't matter what shape you give it. Now visualize this heavy energy exiting through your third eye chakra or energy center. See the energy exit into a clear tube about six inches long. At the end of this tube, visualize a sphere or ball of golden light. Allow all the dark energy in your head to pour out into the tube as if you were pouring water from a facet and direct it into the sphere. Keep releasing energy until you see the color indigo, a deep blue, which is the natural color of this energy center. Now imagine that this sphere at the end of the tube, is Source energy and is transmuting and dissolving the toxic energy. See the toxic energy disappear completely into the light.

Once you feel complete and all the toxic energies from your head has been released, place your hands on your forehead and fill the inside of your head with loving energy. *Yes, you have healing hands!!* Self love heals everything. Most people instantly feel an overwhelming sense of relief.

Today's Higher Idea: When releasing chaotic energy from your body, it is always important to acknowledge the gift or lesson. There is always a reason: for example, your pain may be reminding you to stop watching television that transmits negative or destructive images or to drink more water.

Higher Idea #66 Play the Freedom Movie

Do you see a fearful future full of doom and gloom? Or do you see a future full of abundance, joy and freedom? How you see your future determines the outcome. You determine your future by what you expect to see! I recommend you play the *freedom movie* in your mind to raise your vibration.

Your freedom movie is the movie you play in your mind that casts you in the leading role. This is a great way to train your subconscious mind and help you to expand your awareness of how you view yourself, your beloved, your family, and everyone else in your life. If you want others to show up differently, then I suggest you change the mental image you have of them in your mind. You are in charge of the script, the scenes, and the actors. You are the Divine star, director, and producer. Play the movie of your beautiful life. See yourself living the life you know you can. Visualize every detail, including *being* the person you want to become. This exercise is great because you can release habitual thinking, feelings, and actions that no longer represent the amazing human being that is inside of you. You have the power to change the story line any time to create happy endings.

In order to take responsibility for what you have created in this world, you first need to acknowledge that you are a creator. You create the good, the bad, and the ugly with every thought vibration and the emotional charge attached to it. The good news is that if you are not happy with the life you have created so far, you have the power to change it. You have the power to create beauty, peace, and ultimate freedom.

Your subconscious mind communicates with imagery. It is the imagination that is the connecting link between the invisible and the visible, between the dream and the reality. If you want to train your mind and achieve your dreams, take a moment each day to visualize the YOU already living the life your heart desires. To create the best possible outcome in the next phase of your life, use your imagination and play the movie of *the life you intend on creating* with you as the star.

No matter what dream you visualize, these exercises are about *you*, not a fantasy version of you but the *real* you. What I mean is: Practice seeing yourself in your mind's eye just the way you are right now. This is a powerful practice in self-love and self-acceptance. To appreciate and love the Divine human being you are right now will activate a deeper force within. If you are unable to see yourself in your mind's eye, that is okay. The more you practice, the clearer the image will become. Focus on the greatness that lives within you and your imaginary world will then pull these higher energies into your physical world. The more you visualize what you want to experience, the more you make the unknown *known*, which will empower you in dissolving the fear of the unknown.

Creative imagery is powerful when you add the element of *emotion*. Emotions create the necessary energy, so when you create an imagined reality in your mind and feel as if you are there, your subconscious will believe it to be true and will go about making it so. As you visualize your future, bring in the energy of *joy*. Joy is an attraction magnet and will attract the circumstances and resources you need to make your vision a reality.

When you play your freedom movie, remember to remain focused on creating *your* life. You are not here to influence anyone's journey without permission. So when you visualize, only involve yourself whenever possible. If you bring people you know into your creative dreaming, only see the good. For example, if you are driving home from work and think your spouse/partner will be miserable or unhappy when you get there, then that is what you will experience. Instead, visualize your beloved happy to see you. See yourself giving him/her a hug and letting him/her know you are happy to see him/her. Only project out thoughts and images you want to experience. If you are creating destructive images, then people will feel them energetically in their physical world. We are all connected, so be mindful.

It is not a good idea to stay in dreamland for hours because you do have a life to live. Your present moment requires your full attention, so only spend thirty minutes per day training your subconscious mind to live in freedom. The best time to train your subconscious mind with higher thoughts, words, and images is prior to falling asleep.

Whenever you have moments of losing sight of your dream, play the *freedom movie* in your mind. See and feel yourself living the life you want to live. Visualize yourself being successful because you found a solution to a problem. See yourself uplifting humanity in some way. See yourself as a bestselling author because you have a powerful story of inspiration to share. Consciously creating mental images and feeling yourself there allows you to go beyond your present circumstance.

You may have moments where you have asked the universe, "What the heck is going on?" Welcome to the club. Do not compare your life to anyone else's. Trust that life is working for you behind the scenes. If you are in doubt, have lost your faith, or feel like you are doing all the inner work and still nothing is happening, keep going! Be patient. Recommit to your vision that your heart seeks to experience.

Today's Higher Idea: Play your freedom movie and *embrace* your Joyful Self, your Abundant Self, your Fun Self, your Healthy Self who are here to empower you in living the life you are here to live.

Higher Idea #67 Trust Your Intuition

Has your Intuitive Self become a Forgotten Angel? Your Intuitive Self is the voice of inner knowing. Intuition enables you to define what vibration you are presently in. Your intuition is the voice within that offers you the biggest rewards in life if you choose to listen. Your intuition embodies your divinity or what some refer to as your spirit guides and teachers. Your Intuitive Self is with you now, waiting patiently to assist you in living your Divine purpose, which is the reason why you came to this planet in the first place. The *Divine Mind Conversation* (Higher Idea #79) offers an easy and simple way of connecting to your Intuitive Self and the many Forgotten Angels alive inside of you. You can ask your Intuitive or Brilliant Self to give you guidance at any time.

Although the mind is wondrous, the spiritual dimension connects you to the principles you live by. Connecting to your intuition will give you the courage to explore the dark caverns of your mind, those places of which you were once afraid of. Knowing that you have an inner power that is ready to assist you can bring about a sense of relief and greater trust in your life process. You learn to make the unknown known by expanding your awareness and connecting to your Intuitive Self, which will guide you through uncertainty.

Florence Scovel Shinn wrote in her book, *The Wisdom of Florence Scovel Shinn*, "prayer is telephoning to God and intuition is God telephoning to you. Many people have a busy wire when God telephones and they don't get the message. Your wire is busy when you are discouraged, angry or resentful. Your negative emotions can drown out the voice of intuition."

Today's Higher Idea: Tap your third eye three times and ask your Intuitive Self to help you see more. Now repeat, "I do not have an answer to my problem. I have no idea what to do. I have no idea how I will manifest _____. I am letting go of knowing how it will happen." Take a deep breath in. Now you have allowed your ego to get out of your way and opened the door to your Divine Mind, your Brilliant Self who will bring you the answer or solution you seek.

Higher Idea #68 Imagine the Possibilities of Wealth

As a struggling entrepreneur, I had many moments when I experienced the roller-coaster of feast or famine. With no money in my bank account and not being able to pay my rent, I often thought I was crazy for taking this journey because even though my soul was guiding me to experience all that I was, *love* was not paying the bills. In the moments where I just wanted to pack it all in, my Brilliant Self would remind me, *Wealth is your natural state. Abundance is your natural state. Keep going!*

Money offers physical freedom—the freedom to experience the material world and the pleasures of life. Unfortunately, many wealthy people have material possessions, yet they live very stressful, unhappy lives, and often drown in the drug and alcohol culture. Rich people experience depression and loneliness just like anyone else. What I suggest is to become rich and wealthy on the inside first by connecting with your Forgotten Angels; then you can handle the higher vibrations of unlimited wealth.

For most of my life, I lived in default, allowing my Fallen Angels to control my life. Talk about a roller-coaster ride. At times, I did not understand why I was in the circumstance I was in or why clients were not calling, no matter how much action I took. There were many times I was taken to my knees and had to rely on the kindness of others. I had connected to my Wealthy Self, my Abundant Self, and Worthy Self, and I felt clear and open to these higher vibrations, yet I was not experiencing the sustainable financial wealth I knew I was meant to enjoy. Again, my Brilliant Self would show me an image of my stepfather, smiling and waving hello. Ahh, yes! The message was loud and clear (See Higher Idea #74). Everything was happening for a reason, even if I did not see it in the moment.

My years of experience have taught me that wealth is not about money. Wealth reflects your emotional and mental state. Lack is a state of mind, and wealth is also a state of mind. We are either in poverty consciousness (fear frequency) or wealth consciousness (*Freedom Frequency*). Many of us have been conditioned to believe we do not deserve abundance. Many think that if they have nothing, then they are nothing. On the other end of the spectrum, people may feel that the more material things they have, the more complete they are.

121

When you are vibrating in the Freedom Frequency, you have a wealth of opportunities available to you. You recognize the wealth of friendship, the wealth of family, and the wealth of love in your life. You also have a wealth of creative expression to share with the world.

If you are stuck in the *fear of losing it all* or the *fear of losing control*, you will stop the flow of wealth. Only when you stop beating yourself up and disapproving of yourself can you shift your vibration and attract more abundance. If you have attachments to your possessions, life will teach you to become unattached. We can enjoy all the material things created in the world so long as they do not possess us. Materialism is not meant to control you.

If there is a part of you that believes in *lack,* it is because you are allowing your Lack self (the ego) to control you like a puppet on a string. Your Lack self will have you believe that you are worthless and that you will always have *nothing*. It is time to face your Lack self and take your power back. The Lack self is a Fallen Angel that holds the seed of all lack within you and the more you are afraid of this self or ignore this aspect of you, the more power this *self* has over you. The Lack self only represents one cherry in your Divine cherry pie, and when you have the courage to face this *self* and say, "I will no longer let you control me. I now take my power back!," your life will open up.

As you communicate with your Lack self, you will discover that this *self* was really only lacking *love* from you. That is all any of your Fallen Angels want. As you acknowledge, forgive, and learn how to love this part of you, the negative energetic charge will release. Now you will see your Lack self transform and your Abundant Self will appear. This Forgotten Angel is now remembered, and as you embody these higher vibrations, you align yourself with the infinite supply of abundance, which brings the people, resources and opportunities you require to move forward in your life.

If you do not have the physical freedom to explore externally, then you are being called to explore yourself internally and cultivate the energy of abundance from within. As you transform your internal world and plant new empowering beliefs about yourself, you will release your resistance to shining your light into the external world. The lack of money will also teach you powerful lessons in humility and gratitude so you remain humble and grateful no matter what sphere of reality you are living in.

Many fears begin to surface when the possibility of losing everything is close at hand, such as fear of losing control, fear of loss, fear of pain, fear of the unknown, or fear of what others may think. This is good because now you can release these illusions that have kept you living small. Here you are asked to stay present with the energy and just breathe through it. Remember, your ego will resist the higher idea of you connecting to your, I AM Presence, your Brilliant Self which is already abundant.

Many people attempt to create heaven by surrounding themselves with beautiful things; however, if hell still exists in the mind, you will be living a game you cannot win. Take the time to connect with your Forgotten Angels and integrate with them so you can empower yourself from the inside out.

Today's Higher Idea: Connect to your Wealthy or Abundant Self by imagining that you just won the lottery. It is not about the money, it is the feeling that nothing is missing and you no longer want for anything. Cultivate this energy of abundance and you create a new world for you, your family, and humanity. Say to yourself, "I AM wealth. There is an infinite supply and I am connected to this infinite supply."

Higher Idea #69 Creativity Links You to Abundance

You are here to create! Remember, dreamers and visionaries built this world. Everything that was ever invented from the chair you're sitting on to the clothes you're wearing came through the world of imagination. The world of imagination is very real, and the more you understand how it works, the more ability you have to bring new ideas into this physical world to be experienced.

The material world and the spiritual world are not separate; they are one. If you are afraid of one world, you are also afraid of the other. Explore both worlds and discover the beauty in all creation. We are here to create and share our creations with the world. Money moves the creation process into the material world.

Moving into a higher consciousness of infinite possibilities takes time, so be patient and remember to enjoy your present moment. For example, if you do not appreciate the job you have or you are unhappy in your relationship, flip the idea and view it as your training ground for bigger things to come. Learn the lessons before you and always give the best of yourself. This practice will demonstrate that you have a learning attitude about life. You will know intuitively if and when it is time to move on.

While sitting in meditation is where all my programs, workshops, games, and books were revealed. There is an infinite supply of ideas just waiting to be created and experienced here on earth. Wealth is given to those who create solutions to the world's problems. You have access to an infinite number of creative ideas just waiting to be birthed through you.

Learn to enjoy the creative process of your life. If you *trust* that all your creations are Divinely inspired, then you no longer need to stress out about how you are going to accomplish something or when it must happen.

Today's Higher Idea: If you have created a product or service, let go of the lower idea that you're somehow going to miss out on your piece of the pie or share of the market. This is fear-based thinking. You live in an abundant universe and there is plenty for all. The more you focus on creating value for others and living in gratitude, the more you draw abundance to you. Universal Intelligence will naturally supply you with the right customers or clients who are seeking your products or services.

Higher Idea #70 See the Bigger Picture

If you're uncomfortable with the concept of God, then you are uncomfortable with your own Divinity. When we believe God is just "out there" or a man with a beard in the sky, we immediately create separation. We have made a division between our outer and inner worlds. Some religious followers worship deities outside of themselves, ignoring the internal Source, *the Divine light* within us all.

We have many names for God such as Love, Higher Power, Allah, Universal Intelligence, Divine Mind, Source, Creator, and *Goddess.* The Creator is a concept in virtually every culture in some way. It's important to remember that our Creator is not racist or prejudiced. It is love, abundance, and truth. The Divine Mind is the source of all things; however, when we only see the Creator as *out there*, we may see ourselves as "lesser than" or "just human." It's time to focus on the internal God or Goddess, the Divine Creator within all things and within every one of us.

We often forget that the essence of the Creator moves through us. As I mentioned earlier, a higher idea is to remember that *the God vibration can penetrate your skin.*

We'll never truly know who we are if all we do is idolize what's outside of ourselves. What if you stopped looking up at the heavens and instead looked within. The moment we let go of a particular image of the Creator, we're then able to shift focus and see God as an omnipresent energy penetrating all things. In this way, we're no longer separate from Life. We know we are connected to All That Is. See life from a higher perspective and allow the bigger picture to unfold.

Today's Higher Idea: What if you visualized God, the Source of all things within all things, and knew that every human being is an individualized expression of God, of Universal Intelligence? How differently would you view others? How differently would you see yourself?

Chapter Seven
Integration of Your Divine Mind

Within you is a powerful field of higher intelligence, known as your Divine Mind. Your Divine Mind is the Observer, of the many selves that make up the totality of you. When you enter this unified field of consciousness, you are liberated from the suffering caused by the creations of the fear-based mind, the *ego* and the separation of self.

Each Higher Idea written in this book offers a path to your Divine Mind, an enlightened state of mind where you see yourself as whole and complete. As you integrate all of these higher ideas into your life, you will begin to experience a quantum leap in how you feel inside. You will be vibrating at a higher frequency, allowing your Brilliant Self, the highest version of you, to integrate into your physical body.

As you align with your Divine Mind, your vibration expands with incredible force and everyone is touched by it. Imagination becomes reality and life is unlimited. You discover the art of living. You no longer need to conform to other people's ideas. You are no longer focused on self fulfillment; you are focused on creating value for the greater good. You have a learning attitude and are open to infinite possibilities. You're in the realm of freedom, doing what you love and sharing it with others.

Integration of your Divine Mind takes you beyond the old stories of illness, wrongness, faults, and projections of the fear-based mind. You now remember you are divinely perfect in every moment as you are an expression of All That Is, the Source of all things manifested.

Higher Idea #71 Step Out of the Spiritual Closet

Are you afraid of what others may think of your spiritual beliefs? Spirituality is not a religion, and it's not "New Age." Spirituality is a way of life and is the alignment with Source energy. Spirituality is the devotion toward integrating mind and heart, a journey toward truth.

Many of us have lived in a spiritual closet because we're afraid to be criticized or condemned for our truths. This fear changes as we allow ourselves to listen fully and accept others for who they are even if their spiritual beliefs are not our own. The less you criticize or condemn others for their beliefs, the less you will experience criticism in your own life.

There are times when you play the role of the teacher and times when you play the role of a student. Playing the role of a spiritual guide or teacher requires the skills to explain what you mean with calmness and integrity. Playing the role of a student gives you the space to learn something new that may be very beneficial in the development of your mind and soul. Becoming a student of life means having an open heart and mind as well as a learning attitude. As you devote yourself to the path of higher values, you'll set the standards others will want to follow.

Many eastern philosophies advocate that people are here to spiral up from one plane of consciousness to another. When you are vibrating at a higher frequency, you are often invisible to people functioning in lower vibratory fields, like the *frequency of fear*. The only people you will attract are those who are ready and willing to learn through you, those who are ready to live in the light of self-awareness.

By acknowledging your Divine presence, you become a magnet in the light and no longer need to force or push anything to manifest in your life. Everything begins to unfold naturally and in connection with your soul's purpose.

Today's Higher Idea: Have friends over for dinner and have each person share one thing about her or his spiritual journey that has made a profound difference in her or his life.

Higher Idea #72 Connect to Your Brilliant Self

What would be your response be if someone asked you, "What motivates you to do the things you do or say the things you say?" Many people respond to this question with the statement, "I don't know. I just do what I do." We tend to go through life on automatic pilot, buying this, doing that, saying this, and at times, being completely unaware of the motivating factor behind our words or actions.

As I mentioned earlier, a powerful universal force flows through you. If you acknowledge this Divine intelligence, you'll activate the opening of spiritual channels that allow you to communicate and receive higher wisdom. You come to know that everything in life progresses through experience.

You are here to recognize the Divine power that spirals through you. The light of your soul remains hidden until you acknowledge it with your conscious mind. Only then will your soul reawaken and lead you out of the fear frequency into the light of truth—the truth of who you are.

Higher worlds of love are obtained through disciplining the mind, emotional integrity, and a strong spiritual connection. Powerful tools for opening the heart and connecting you to the spiritual dimension are:

- Meditation – connects you to your feeling center.

- Deep Breathing – connects you to life force energy.

- Trusting Your Intuition – connects you to your inner wisdom.

- Healthy Imagination – connects you to your creativity.

You also connect to the spiritual dimension through empowering others. Lifting others up will bring you joy and a greater sense of belonging in the world. It's important to remember to assist only those who are ready to wake up to the truth; otherwise, you'll exhaust yourself by trying to force others to see or feel what they may not be ready to grasp.

The spiritual energy that flows through you will also empower you to solve every problem, no matter how big. Connecting to Universal intelligence is achieved by raising your consciousness. Consciousness refers to the level of awareness of who you are, the life you have created, and the reality you live in.

Your journey on earth becomes less complicated, stressful, and chaotic when you make every effort to connect with your Forgotten Angels. The more you lighten up your mind and physical body (the temple of your soul), the more you see that the path you are on is divinely perfect. When you are connected to your Divine Intelligence, your Brilliant Self, you no longer need to fear for your safety. You will always be guided to the right place at the right time.

Today's Higher Idea: Ask yourself, "Does my Fearful self control my mind or does my Brilliant Self guide me?" A powerful exercise is to visualize the knowledge of the Universe as liquid golden light entering the top of your head, filling your brain, and spiraling down into every cell of your body. With every breath, you ask your cells to awaken and activate your soul's blueprint.

Higher Idea #73 Be of Service to Others

Being of service is about giving without any expectation of receiving something in return. It is unconditional *giving* and at the same time there is no giving when you are in the Freedom Frequency. You are simply flowing universal energy to the one who is before you. You are aware of what needs to be done and offer your energy from a place of ease and grace. Selfless service is about honoring the Divine presence in each and every human being.

Being of service is a wonderful spiritual practice. Here you can identify whether you are giving from a place of divine essence or giving because the ego wants to be recognized. If you are giving so others can see that you are giving, then you are giving from the place of, "Look at how good I am." Selfless service is from the heart and needs no acknowledgement.

You can be of service to your beloved, your family, to a group or community or cause. Being of service involves connecting to what matters to you most. A conscious entrepreneur creates a business to help solve a problem and to be of service to the world. We are all here to make a difference and harmonically collaborate.

In the Freedom Frequency, you no longer place yourself above others and you no longer see others on a pedestal. Instead of thinking, "What's in it for me?" your *focus* is on how you can make a difference and add value to the lives of others.

Being of service should not cost you way more than you can afford financially, physically, spiritually or emotionally. Being in a high vibration of health and well being is important if you want to serve others in the best way possible.

Remember, no one can take advantage of you unless you let them. True happiness and ultimate freedom are measured by how much you give, not by what you receive. However, when you give from the heart, you expand your capacity to receive more joy and fulfillment in your life.

Today's Higher Idea: Become aware of the self within that asks, "What is in it for me?" Let this inner Fallen Angel know this attitude is no longer acceptable and you are now reframing your question to, "What can I do to make a positive difference in someone's life today?"

Higher Idea #74 Listen to Your Brilliant Self

I have a true story I want to share with you. I love travelling so a few years ago I planned a road trip to Arizona with a man I was living with at the time. I had been to Arizona a few years earlier with a girlfriend and had fallen in love with the beauty of the desert.

As I was sitting at my computer planning our trip, I heard a voice in my head that said, "Take your mom and John (stepdad) on the trip." I ignored the voice at first because I wanted to make this a romantic road trip with my guy. My Brilliant Self was persistent and kept repeating the words, "Take your mom and John on the trip," until I took action and called my mom. I asked her whether she and John wanted to travel with us to Arizona. Delighted with the idea, they said, "Yes." Within a few weeks, we were off on our two-week road trip from Calgary to Phoenix. My mom and John were the perfect travel companions, and even though they were both seniors, they acted like excited children, laughing and enjoying every moment. They explored the Grand Canyon and took their first ever helicopter tour in Sedona to celebrate my mom's seventy-second birthday. But what was truly amazing was that there was not one argument between the four us the entire trip.

About six months later, my Brilliant Self said the exact same words again: "Take your mom and John on a trip." Well, this time I had not planned to go anywhere but I remembered that my mom and John had purchased a time-share. Again, I ignored the voice because I was busy creating my website for my coaching business and did not have the time or budget to go anywhere. Or so I thought. Again, my Brilliant Self was persistent so I called my mom and asked whether they wanted to go on another trip. Well, my mom immediately said that she had an aunt and a cousin in Pasadena whom she would love to see. My Brilliant Self knew that I loved empowering people and making their dreams come true, so I booked a flight, and within a week, my mom, John, and I were flying to Los Angeles for a week's holiday.

On this trip, I discovered many things about my stepdad, John. I found out that he had never worn shorts or running shoes. I was totally amazed, but then knowing him, I quickly understood. He was an eighty-year-old Scottish gentleman who always dressed sharply. To our surprise, he actually bought himself a pair of walking shorts and running shoes. He just laughed when he saw his legs and joked about how white they were.

Driving down the coast, I was drawn to pull over at a beach parking lot. I suggested to my parents that we go for a walk along the beach. We all took our shoes off, walked across the sand, and walked in the water.

As I took pictures of Mom and John laughing like children, I realized my stepdad had tears in his eyes. When I asked him whether he was okay, he said, "In my eighty years, I have never felt the ocean on my toes before."

We had many *firsts* on that trip, and I was so glad once again to have followed through with the wisdom of my Remembered Angel.

Two months later, guess what? The voice, again! Yes, I was hearing the exact same words: "Take your parents on a trip.*" This time I listened, and I felt drawn to invite my whole family, which included my boyfriend, brother Dwayne, my mom, and John, as well as my dad and my stepmom. And yes, both sets of parents are great friends, which is an amazing story in itself.

I organized and planned a four-day trip for all seven of us to fly to New York City to experience the Big Apple together. My brother Dwayne and I had been to New York several times, attending tradeshows over the years, but this was a first for everyone else. We laughed, cried, and deepened our connections over a dinner harbor tour, awed by the architecture, and enjoyed the amazing sights of Manhattan.

Again, two months later, I was sitting at my computer writing when once more my Brilliant Self said, "Take your parents on a trip." It may sound a little crazy, but I had learned to listen to my Brilliant Self, even if I did not know the reason in the moment.

So I called my mom and John and asked whether they wanted to travel to California and spend her seventy-third birthday in Santa Barbara. They immediately said, "Yes", so the three of us were off for another adventure. I chauffeured them up the coast to a beautiful resort where we wined and dined, laughed till we cried, relaxed, and rejuvenated. I was amazed with the transformation that had taken place within my stepdad over the past year because I had known him to have quite the temper. He was embracing his Humorous Self as he had us laughing for hours, and he also embraced his Generous Self, not letting me pay for anything.

A week after arriving home, my mom called to ask me whether we could go to Hawaii on our next trip. I love Hawaii, so I was thrilled with their choice of a tropical destination. When I hung up the phone, I sat for a moment and realized I did not have the same sense of urgency as I had experienced when planning previous trips. I did not hear the words I had become so use to hearing from my Brilliant Self. Within a month, I discovered why. My stepfather had just been diagnosed with leukemia, and within a week, he passed away.

I share this incredible experience with you to encourage you to always listen to your voice of intuition, even if it doesn't make sense. Your Brilliant Self always knows what is best for you and others, and if you listen, you are sure to be guided on an amazing adventure.

I am so grateful that I took the time to listen. I got to see and experience in a completely different way a man I had known for many years. These trips were a blessing for all of us and I have memories I will always cherish. Just hours before he passed away, my stepdad took my hand, tears in both our eyes, and he said, *"Karen, thank you for giving me the best year of my life."*

Six months later, I took my mom to Maui, Hawaii and we were given many gifts from spirit.

Higher Idea #75 You Live in an Abundant Universe

Since money is man-made, why is it that we (humanity) need, crave, and will do almost anything to have this man-made product? Why are people judged if they do not have man/woman made products (materialism)? If we have no money in our bank accounts, why is it we are deemed *failures*? Why do we link money to our self-worth?

These are powerful questions, and now more than ever, we are beginning to realize that self-worth has nothing to do with what we have in our bank accounts or in achievements. If the financial system crashed, would that mean we were all worthless? No. Self-worth is realized when you are connected to the true source of abundance. The true source of abundance is not money, your employer, your clients or customers. The true source of abundance is God, your I AM presence, the Source, the Universe, Creator, or whatever name you give this Infinite Intelligence. The God Vibration flows through every human being and throughout all of life, and it is the source of all wealth, health, wisdom, love, joy, prosperity, creativity, abundance, and miracles.

There is an infinite supply of resources and opportunities available for every human being. Yes, you can actually have what you want, knowing that no one will be deprived of getting what they want. This is how abundant our universe is. If you listen to your inner Fallen Angels that say, "I am not worthy; I do not deserve more; there isn't enough" or "I will go last to make sure everyone gets what they want," then these beliefs will disconnect you from the Source and separate you from the infinite supply of abundance.

You may have wondered, "If this is an abundant universe, then why are so many people suffering in poverty and children dying of hunger?" This question is not easily answered; however, we do not know the journey of each soul and the life lessons it is to experience. There are many powerful souls on this planet that have made a choice to come to earth and live for a short time, or in poverty or play out a victim role so others can learn valuable life lessons through them, such as compassion, love, and selfless service. I was once on welfare, but now I am an author and founder of a global women's organization. Who knew? The best advice I can offer is to send others your blessings and love and then bring the focus back on you. Change your life first so you can be the example of what is possible.

If your vibration resonates in fear, you will block yourself from receiving the abundance that is only a frequency away. Spiraling up and out of the worlds of lack or a poverty consciousness involves mental, emotional, and spiritual discipline and devotion. As you expand and create wealth within your mind and trust that there is more than enough for everyone, you will begin to experience a world that is full of resources, opportunities, love, support, food, and money. It is your wealth frequency, living above the line, that will draw these things into your life.

As I mentioned in Higher Idea #69, it is your creativity, the divine gift within, that you are here to share with the world. When you are connected to Infinite Source, you will be guided to meet the people who are seeking what you offer.

Trust that you are always provided with exactly what you need at the right time. The more you tune into the Freedom Frequency, the more you tune into an abundant life. All that is required is remembering the truth—that you are worthy and are here on this planet to enjoy the best life has to offer.

Today's Higher Idea: Ask and you shall receive. Focus on how you would feel if you had everything you wanted. Say to yourself, "I live in an abundant universe and there is plenty for all of us."

Higher Idea #76 We Are All One

Many of us have become divided in our thoughts, creating separation or *duality* in our daily life experiences. Now we can truly recognize that the fear frequency isn't separate from the Freedom Frequency. It's a mirror reflection. The frequencies are just at opposite ends of the spectrum. They're like two sides of a coin. We cannot have freedom unless we have experienced its opposite. Once we thoroughly understand fear and embrace the gift, we see that the only thing left is the truth of our existence. Nothing is separate; we are all mirrors of each other expressing our own unique and creative selves.

This book focuses on the duality of fear and freedom, the dark and the light to show you how divided you may have become within your own mind. This division, however, is only for the sake of learning and identifying the energies that are alive inside of you. Once you come to terms with what fear is—*the ultimate illusion*—it transforms, and all that remains is the truth—that only *love* is real.

You recognize that all chaos, tragedy, trauma, change, or destruction bring the necessary adjustments required to manifest higher energy vibrations in the Freedom Frequency of life.

We have chosen to see fear and freedom as being in two different places. We have chosen to see our emotions and our life as good or bad, positive or negative, and right or wrong. The polarity of third dimensional living is dissolving as we spiral up into higher dimensions and remember that at the core of all existence is LOVE, *enlightened love*. Enlightened love is the Divine glue that unifies everything.

When you let go of duality *within*—the good and bad perspectives—and consciously choose to see only the unity and perfection of All That Is, your life harmonizes.

When we begin to believe that we have learned everything we can from the world of pain and suffering, which is ultimately the separation of our own Divine nature, we will spiral up out of fear-based living. We have ignored, forgotten, resisted, and feared who we are long enough. We are waking up and remembering that we collectively created this earthly experience and all its contrasts. We're all brothers and sisters on an earthly journey, and it's time to come home to ourselves. It's time for all of us to breathe in unity and see the Divine plan in all its magnificence.

As we integrate the divine masculine and divine feminine energies that flow through us, we see heaven within our own mind which is then reflected out into our experience. As we send love to all the creatures that inhabit this beautiful planet, we embrace global love. By loving and appreciating the Earth, dissolving ideas of winners or losers, knowing that we're all gifted human beings, releasing fear of one another, integrating darkness into light, serving and uplifting everyone around us, we birth *unity and unite in universal love.*

The *Freedom Frequency* is embodying your Divine nature. When you have internal freedom, you experience external freedom. Spirit is calling you to explore your inner worlds and acknowledge your Fallen and Forgotten Angels so you can integrate and become ONE, the Remembered Angel.

You no longer need to learn from fear. You are complete. You are now remembering who you are and letting go of all you are *not* so you may emerge with the highest expression of who you are. Now, together, we create heaven on earth.

Today's Higher Idea: Embrace your divinity by sending loving thought vibrations out to all the children of earth.

Higher Idea #77 See the Divine Order in Your Life

At the core of all things, at their vibratory level, is absolute perfect order. This means that at the core of who you are is *Divine Intelligence.*

Your power is in the present moment. Only when you are present can you see the Divine order of life. Even when things appear at their worst, there is Divine order. For example, when doors of opportunity and abundance close, it is usually a sign that you are being called to go within and shift your internal world. Once *thought adjustments* are made and you are in Divine alignment, the supply of abundance will reopen its doors once again. Order and flow are always restored.

When you're vibrating in the Freedom Frequency, you will never experience loneliness because you remember that you are not alone. You may experience aloneness, which is very different than feeling lonely. In the reality of this freedom, you no longer have a need to escape circumstances. You make the choice to experience the moment fully and to embrace the fullness.

When you recognize the Divine order of life, you will trust that you're the right person in the right place at the right time and engaged in exactly what you're meant to be doing in that moment. Trust that when the money runs out, more money will appear, or when one project fails, another project will show up, or when an opportunity is missed, another door will open. As you flow in thoughts of abundance, life flows along with you.

Today's Higher Idea: How will you spark your divinity today?

Higher Idea #78 Breathe in the Light

Shining your light, your love onto the world, involves opening your heart and giving of yourselves. Some people mistakenly believe that if they *give,* they won't have. It's not about being a martyr and forgetting about your own needs. The kind of giving I'm referring to is empowering others to help make their dreams come true, whether it's giving advice, energy, direction, financial assistance, or most importantly, our time. Our attitude of self-gratification is transformed when we consider others and show them we truly care.

Light is love! When you are no longer afraid of your light, then you are living on purpose which is to be the *light* that you are, the *love* that you are and share your vibration with the world. Some people may not understand or accept the journey you're on. You may be laughed at, ignored, gossiped about, yelled at, and told to stop dreaming foolish dreams and to get a real job. Some people may even stop loving you. On the path to living above the line, some may even tell you that you'll never make it; even some of your friends may not believe in you. Will any of this stop you? Remember, a person with a mission in life will ignore those who seek to instill fear and doubt. A person who lives with purpose will only listen to those who inspire and give encouragement. Keep refining, enhancing, and expressing your vision.

If the satellites in the sky focused on you, they would see a light so bright that those viewing the images would think it was a small city. You have a star inside of you just waiting for the moment to shine brightly for all to see. A star's journey is never an overnight success. Whether you want to perform for others or create products or services that uplift humanity, it's up to you. Just live with an open heart and your life will be prosperous. Remember the movie *Pay It Forward*? That's one of my favorite movies because I believe if we have the courage to spread our light, we open ourselves up to a new way of living and being.

Today's Higher Idea: Shine your light, your love on everyone you meet from this day forward.

Higher Idea #79 Divine Mind Conversations

Many people have a difficult time approaching issues or problems in their relationships or in their business due to their fear of conflict. They have developed the belief that, "If I talk about this issue, I will become disappointed or I will disappoint others or I will be criticized." Unresolved issues eventually magnify over time causing resentment, blame, and disconnection.

The *Divine Mind Conversation* was designed to transform the relationship you have with yourself so you can transform the relationships you have with others. It is a powerful tool you can use to face issues in your life without having to face the person directly. This process shifts the negative energetic charge you have toward others and yourself and prepares you for healthy emotional expression so you can approach anyone, talk about anything and at the same time, keep your vibration above the line.

So how does it work? As I mentioned earlier, it is best to have a facilitator guide you through the first time so you are completely aware of the steps involved. You are working with a very intelligent source that lives inside of you, and it must be contained and approached with the deepest of respect. Skipping steps will not give you the desired results. If steps are taken with guidance, the end result is a direct experience of enlightenment (*lightening up*).

The *Divine Mind Conversation* was shown to me in meditation many years ago to assist me in discovering deeper parts of myself I did not know existed. If it was true that my invisible worlds—my mental, emotional, and spiritual dimensions—created my physical experience, then I knew that if I were to transform my life, I had to find a way to communicate with these invisible aspects of myself.

The *Divine Mind Conversation* is a seven step process that combines creative imagery and self-hypnosis. The complete experience is realized through your imagination. Here you become consciously aware of the sensations in the body that either react or respond to images appearing in your mind. Your imagination offers you insight (*inner sight*) to see beyond your five senses. If you think you will have a hard time seeing or imagining images within your mind because you haven't been able to in the past, that is okay. Magic seems to happen as the pineal gland

140

activates, giving you the ability to see full color pictures even if you have never been able to before.

The *Divine Mind Conversation* will empower you to see yourself from many different angles of reflection. You will know the process is working when the images you are creating cause tears to surface or tingles in your body. You may feel uncomfortable as truth emerges. Then a rush of energy bursts through offering relief and potentially freedom as you now accept and see yourself from a completely new perspective. These are all signs that the process is shifting your internal worlds and releasing negative energy that no longer serves you.

Below is a very brief summary of the seven steps involved in.

Step One – Enter your Divine Mind. The *Divine Mind Conversation* begins with imagining a mansion in your Divine Mind, the unified field of consciousness. You then open the door and enter into a white room known as the Purification Room. This space is infused with the highest vibration, *enlightened love*. Here, any and all dark and negative thoughts, ideas, or forces that create separation are dissolved and transmuted. In this room is a table and three chairs. Two chairs on one side of the room for you and your Brilliant Self (the highest version of who you are) and the third chair is on the other side of the table.

Step Two – Meet Your Fallen Angel. Now bring forth *one* inner Fallen Angel that is causing you the most problems in your life and have them sit across from you. Sometimes it is easier to begin with visualizing someone in your life with whom you have a lot of unresolved anger with. If you have a negative association with any family member, friend, or co-worker, then that person has become a Fallen Angel in your mind.

Step Three – Express All Incomplete Communication. Here you have an opportunity to transform your emotional pain by directing and expressing all the unspoken communication and the truth of how you feel onto the Fallen Angel that sits before you. Give yourself permission to vent with your inner voice instead of your outer voice, which releases all the pent up negative energy that has been suppressed. Whatever you express within your Divine Mind, such as anger, rage, hate, or sadness, in this inner realm, it is instantly transmuted and dissolved into the light without any karmic effect occurring in your physical reality. Do not hold back any emotion. Stay here until the energy in your body has neutralized or you feel relieved, lighter, or liberated. Take a deep breath!

Step Four – Become the Observer. Now it is your turn to listen and feel the power of vulnerability by giving your Fallen Angel a voice and listening to every word. Yes, they will express words you have been afraid to hear in your outer life. Some words may shock you. Just breathe deeply and slowly. Learning to listen and observe without taking it personally is the practice. All words are transmuted in the realm of Divine Mind as love is the greatest power. As you observe, you will begin to see that it is only your inner Fallen Angels that hold the seed of anger, or frustration, or hate, or the seed of stress, and so on. Once you recognize and completely understand that the anger, stress, frustration, or any perceived negative emotion you experience, does not come from any external source, you are *enlightened*. The negative emotions or states only come from the mind, from the inner intelligence of a Fallen Angel. Listen with compassion and have a learning attitude. Breathe deeply!

Step Five - Forgive Your Fallen Angels. You begin to shift your vibration when you no longer believe what your Fallen Angels are saying is true. It is their story and you are only here to acknowledge and not judge what they say as wrong or right, good or bad. If you attempt to kick out, throw out, or banish a Fallen Angel, its energy will strengthen. It is your love and forgiveness that will dissolve the negative energetic charge associated with each Fallen Angel. Now you can say within your mind, "Thank you for meeting me here. I am so sorry it took so long for me to see you, hear you and acknowledge you. Please forgive me."

Step Six – Be Open To Receiving the Gift. Every inner self has a divine message for you that can assist you in moving forward. Once the energy projected from your Fallen Angel has neutralized, you can let them know the truth that they are loved and accepted by you. Ask the Fallen Angel before you, "What message do you have for me? What is it you need from me?" Now Listen. Can you commit to their request? Remember, their request must serve your highest good.

Step Seven – Walk into the Light of Integration. Once you have received the message, say, "Thank you", and then visualize both of you walking through a door and leaving the room of your Divine Mind. You are now in a beautiful garden standing in the sunlight, the light of integration, the light of knowing you have the power to transform darkness into light. Take 3 deep belly breathes. And so it is.

Higher Idea #80 You Are the Remembered Angel

The *Divine Mind Conversations* will show you how to stop projecting your negative emotions outwardly toward others and to *turn around* and go within to face your Fallen Angels in the white room of your Divine Mind.

The *Divine Mind Conversation* is a powerful tool to bring forth all your inner Forgotten Angels who will assist you in vibrating at a higher frequency. Once you acknowledge each Forgotten Angel such as your Passionate Self, your Happy Self, your Grateful Self, your Joyful Self, your Wealthy Self, your Wise Self, your Healthy Self, and so on, they transform into Remembered Angels. These positive or higher qualities live inside of you, and it is up to you to integrate all these higher vibrations so you can spiral up and live above the line.

Yes, you have the power to transform and release all negative emotions and limited beliefs. Through the process of using your imagination and your emotions to *feel* everything, you release your Fallen Angels into the light and integrate all your Forgotten Angels that offer the riches of life.

Over time as you continue this practice, you will know you are complete when all the voices that hold a negative energetic charge have left the building, the mansion of your Divine Mind. When all voices have become unified, you will be standing with the one voice, the voice of your Brilliant Self.

You are meant to live above the line in the frequency of love, *enlightened love.* You are not your fear. You are not your beliefs. You are not your emotions. You are not your body. You are remembering that all the angels that live inside of you are to be integrated. Each angel symbolizes an "angle of light" that you are here to reflect. You are here to integrate each one until you are left with only ONE angel—YOU!

You are the ONE we have been waiting for.

The REMEMBERED Angel!

Whole and complete.

Here to create heaven on earth.

143

From the Author

There comes a moment in everyone's life where all the pieces of the puzzle join together and the lines vanish. The life picture you once dreamt about is clear and unfolding before you. Finally! You realize all the effort you've put into disciplining your emotional, mental, spiritual, and physical dimensions as well as everything in between was well worth it. It's as if all the planets and stars have aligned and now your dreams have become reality.

The most important question I want you to remember is: *Where are you vibrating—fear or freedom?* Awareness of your energetic vibration is key to living above the line. Remember, your thoughts and emotions are constantly sending out vibrations in every moment. Your brain is a transmitter of your energy signature, and it is constantly emitting a signal out into the field of life.

Living in freedom is embracing all of life. When you do, all the suffering, challenges, struggles, failures, deceptions, and lower vibratory worlds completely vanish. You sit on top of your mountain, viewing life for the first time from a new vantage point. You understand that everything you went through during the climb to higher consciousness was there to show you the path home to yourself. Every experience was necessary and perfectly orchestrated.

Remember, you've spent years preparing yourself for this world of freedom. As you settle into the new life you've designed, you know to say, "Yes" when life presents you with an opportunity.

The development of your mind and soul is your responsibility;

ultimately, your destiny is in your hands. Living in the Freedom Frequency is your Divine power to transform all relationships and your life.

The world of fear will still exist around you. People you encounter and the many forms of mass media will constantly remind you of other realities. Discover your own truths. Keep your focus on creating heaven on earth for you, your family, your community, and the world.

I trust that after reading these pages, you're *fired up* about life! I feel this book represents a piece of my own life's puzzle. I have held back in publishing this book for many years. Now I say, "YES" as I shine my light out into the world to connect with you.

I honor you as you shine your light and make the choice to live in the Freedom Frequency of life. Enjoy the journey home, the journey home to your heart.

Spiral up and fly high.

Karen Klassen

Recommended Resources

❖ The mission of the Institute of HeartMath is to help establish heart-based living and global coherence by inspiring people to connect with the intelligence and guidance of their own hearts. Receive free tools and resources by visiting **www.heartmath.org**

❖ *New York Times* best-selling author Gregg Braden is internationally renowned as a pioneer in bridging science, spirituality, and the real world. **www.gregbraden.com**

❖ Dr. Bradley Nelson, a renowned holistic physician and author of *The Emotion Code*, reveals how emotionally-charged events from your past can still be haunting you in the form of "trapped emotions" around the heart. www.drbradleynelson.com/

❖ Raise your vibration with the power of music and sound. Sound Wellness offers many resources in healing your mind, body and spirit. **www.soundwellness.com**

❖ Thoughts and words carry a vibration that can either destroy or create harmony. Thanks to the experimental work of Dr. Masaru Emoto, we can look to water, and its crystals, to confirm the transformative power of beautiful music, positive thinking, uplifting speech, and prayer. www.masaru-emoto.net

- ❖ David Wolfe is a Health, Nutrition and Superfood Expert. Information on high vibrational foods and the benefits of eating raw food are available at: **http://www.longevitywarehouse.com**

- ❖ The documentary *Project Forgive* focuses on authentic stories that dive into the emotionally mature conversation of forgiveness to cause a global shift in consciousness. The project is a deep inquiry that questions: What does it really mean to forgive? Why can some forgive easily, while others struggle? What happens to us physiologically, spiritually, and emotionally when we forgive? What happens when we don't? **www.projectforgive.com**

- ❖ If you are a woman who is ready to awaken and embody her divine feminine or bring more spirituality into her business, relationships and life, join our sisterhood. **www.womenembracingbrilliance.com**

- ❖ If you are a man who is ready to be remarkable in all areas of your life. **www.remarkablemanproject.com**

- ❖ The *Divine Mind Conversation* and the Emotional Integrity Process is available at **www.karenklassen.ca**

Silent No More

In meditation I fly
Stumbling upon the truths that are I
The light is so bright inside
I cannot hide
I accept my lessons
Learn to apply
Experiences of unpleasantness I face
Becoming one with dignity and grace

Mother Gaia I have known
In every life I have been born
To seek the wisdom from within
I have the answers.
I create
To become one with Source is never too late

Love is the key
To the door once closed in me
In the cycle of life
In the journey of remembering
To find I AM Divine perfection

I can no longer remain silent
For my brothers and sisters
Awake from your sleep
It is now time to go within, go deep, go deep
The heart, the soul does call
There we find our connectedness to all

By Karen Klassen

About the Author

Karen Klassen is founder of Women Embracing Brilliance, a global sisterhood dedicated to empowering women to expand their capacities to receive optimal health, experience a higher love and prosperity by embracing their Divine feminine power. Karen is a creator and facilitator of the Brilliant Heart Beautiful Life Program for women available at **www.womenembracingbrilliance.com**

Karen offers the *Divine Mind Conversation* Series of guided meditations to Brilliant and Beautiful Life Members of Women Embracing Brilliance available at **www.womenembracingbrilliance.com**

Karen is an inspirational speaker and an Enlightened Love coach who reminds you that there is a higher love and wisdom within you that can dissolve all mental, emotional, and physical pain so you can integrate with the highest version of who you.

If you have any questions or are interested in attending the Freedom Frequency Intensive workshops or have private coaching sessions with Karen Klassen, please contact her at **www.karenklassen.ca**

CPSIA information can be obtained at www.ICGtesting.com
Printed in the USA
LVOW10s0032220813

349010LV00018B/344/P